Editorial Project Manager
Eric Migliaccio

Editor in Chief
Karen J. Goldfluss, M.S. Ed.

Cover Artist
Sarah Kim

Illustrator
Clint McKnight

Art Coordinator
Renée Mc Elwee

Imaging
James Edward Grace
Amanda R. Harter

Publisher
Mary D. Smith, M.S. Ed.

CLOSE
Text-Dependent
Questions

THE TEXTS
☑ Short
☑ Complex
☑ High-Interest

THE TASKS
☑ Read and reread
☑ Summarize
☑ Annotate
☑ Collaborate
☑ Ask and answer
☑ Cite and support

THE TDQS
☑ Key details
☑ Word choices
☑ Structure
☑ Purpose
☑ Inference
☑ Opinion

Success!

Teacher Created Resources

Author
Ruth Foster, M.Ed.

For the Lexile measures of the reading passages included in this book, visit *www.teachercreated.com* and click on the Lexile Measures button located on this resource's product page.

For correlations to the Common Core State Standards, see pages 95–96 of this book or visit *http://www.teachercreated.com/standards*.

Teacher Created Resources, Inc.
12621 Western Avenue
Garden Grove, CA 92841
www.teachercreated.com
ISBN: 978-1-4206-2738-1

© 2017 Teacher Created Resources, Inc.
Made in U.S.A.

Teacher Created Resources

Table of Contents

Overview

What Is Close Reading?

Close reading is thoughtful, critical analysis of a text. Close-reading instruction gives your students guided practice in approaching, understanding, and, ultimately, mastering complex texts. This type of instruction builds positive reading habits and allows students to successfully integrate their prior experiences and background knowledge with the unfamiliar text they are encountering.

There are certain factors that differentiate close-reading instruction from other types of reading instruction. These factors include the types of **texts** used for instruction, the **tasks** students are asked to perform, and the **questions** they are expected to answer. For detailed information on these factors, see "A Closer Look" on pages 4–5.

What Are Text-Dependent Questions?

Text-dependent questions (TDQs) can only be answered by referring explicitly back to the text. They are designed to deepen the reader's understanding of the text, and they require students to answer in such a way that higher-level thinking is demonstrated. To be most effective, TDQs should address all that a reading passage has to offer; the questions asked should prompt students to consider the meaning, purpose, structure, and craft contained within the text.

How Is This Guide Organized?

The units in *Close Reading with Text-Dependent Questions* are divided into two sections. Each of the twenty **Section I Units** (pages 8–87) is a four-page unit.

Page 1 **Close-Reading Passage**	This page contains a short, complex, high-interest reading passage. Parts of the passage are numbered for easy reference, and space for annotation is provided in the left margin and between lines of text.
Page 2 **Close-Reading Tasks**	Students are guided to read the passage, summarize it, reread and annotate it, and meet with a partner to discuss and define the author's word choices.
Page 3 **Text-Dependent Questions**	Students are asked to display a general understanding of the text, locate key details within it, cite evidence, and begin to use tools such as inference.
Page 4 **More TDQs**	Students examine the structure of the text and the author's purpose. They form opinions and use evidence to support and defend claims. A research prompt encourages choice, exploration, and cross-curricular connections. (**Note:** Monitor students' Internet research for content appropriateness.)

Each of the two **Section II Units** (pages 88–91) contains two pages.

Page 1 **Close-Reading Passage**	This page contains a short, complex, high-interest reading passage. Parts of the passage are numbered for easy reference, and space for annotation is provided in the left margin and between lines of text.
Page 2 **Peer-Led Tasks**	This page guides groups of students through a series of peer-led tasks in which each member is assigned a different role. Students become teachers to one another as they work together to analyze a text.

A Closer Look

Close Reading with Text-Dependent Questions focuses on the three main components of close-reading instruction: the **texts** students are asked to read, the **tasks** they are instructed to perform, and the **text-dependent questions (TDQs)** they are expected to answer thoughtfully and accurately.

The Texts

✓ short
✓ complex
✓ high-interest
✓ multi-genre

Not all texts are appropriate for close-reading instruction. Passages need to be written in a manner that invites analysis and at a level that requires slow, careful, deliberate reading. The texts in this guide achieve these goals in a number of ways.

- **Length:** Close-reading passages should be relatively short because the rigorous work required of students could make longer passages overwhelming.

Each unit in this guide contains a one-page passage of about 375–400 words. This is an ideal length to introduce and explore a subject, while allowing students of this age to conduct an in-depth examination of its content and purpose.

- **Complexity:** The best way to foster close reading of informational or fictional text is through text complexity. Writing achieves a high level of text complexity when it fulfills certain factors. The **purpose** of the text is implicit or hidden in some way, and the **structure** of the text is complex and/or unconventional. The **demands** of the text ask students to use life experiences, cultural awareness, and content knowledge to supplement their understanding. The **language** of the text incorporates domain-specific, figurative, ironic, ambiguous, or otherwise unfamiliar vocabulary.

The passages in this guide contain all of these different types of language and ask students to decipher their meanings in the context of the parts (words, phrases, sentences, etc.) around them. The passages meet the purpose and structure criteria by delaying key information, defying reader expectations, and/or including unexpected outcomes — elements that challenge students to follow the development of ideas along the course of the text. Students must combine their prior knowledge with the information given in order to form and support an opinion.

- **Interest:** Since close reading requires multiple readings, it is vital that the topics covered and style employed be interesting and varied. The passages in this resource will guide your students down such high-interest avenues as adventure, invention, discovery, and oddity. These texts are written with humor and wonder, and they strive to impart the thrill of learning.

- **Text Types and Genres:** It is important to give students experience with the close reading of a wide variety of texts. The passages in this guide are an equal mix of fiction and nonfiction; and they include examples and/or combinations of the following forms, text types, and genres: drama, poetry, descriptive, narrative, expository, and argumentative.

- **Lexile-Leveled:** A Lexile measure is a quantitative tool designed to represent the complexity of a text. The passages featured in this resource have been Lexile-leveled to ensure their appropriateness for this grade level. For more information, visit this resource's product page at *www.teachercreated.com.*

A Closer Look (cont.)

The Tasks

- ✓ read and reread
- ✓ summarize
- ✓ annotate
- ✓ collaborate
- ✓ connect
- ✓ illustrate
- ✓ cite and support
- ✓ ask and answer

An essential way in which close-reading instruction differs from other practices can be seen in the tasks students are asked to perform. This resource focuses on the following student tasks:

- **Read and Reread:** First and foremost, close reading requires multiple readings of the text. This fosters a deeper understanding as the knowledge gained with each successive reading builds upon the previous readings. To keep students engaged, the tasks associated with each reading should vary. When students are asked to reread a passage, they should be given a new purpose or a new group of questions that influences that reading.

- **Annotation:** During at least one reading of the passage, students should annotate, or make notes on, the text. Annotation focuses students' attention on the text and allows them to track their thought processes as they read. It also allows students to interact with the text by noting words, phrases, or ideas that confuse or interest them. When writing about or discussing a text, students can consult their annotations and retrieve valuable information.

> For more information about annotation, see pages 6–7 of this guide.

- **Additional Tasks:** Collaboration allows students to discuss and problem-solve with their partner peers. An emphasis is placed on demonstrating an understanding of unfamiliar words in context and applying academic vocabulary in new ways. Throughout, students are prompted to cite evidence to support claims and reinforce arguments. Often, students are asked to illustrate written information or connect text to visuals. A section of peer-led activities (pages 88–91) encourages students to ask and answer peer-generated questions.

The TDQs

- ✓ general
- ✓ key details
- ✓ word choice
- ✓ sequence
- ✓ structure
- ✓ purpose
- ✓ inference
- ✓ opinion

Text-dependent questions (TDQs) emphasize what the text has to offer as opposed to the students' personal experiences. This helps students focus on the text — from the literal (what it says) to the structural (how it works) to the inferential (what it means).

The TDQs in this resource ask students to demonstrate a wide range of understanding about the text. There is a progression from questions that ask for general understanding to those that require deeper levels of focus. The first question or two are relatively easy to answer, as this promotes student confidence and lessens the possibility for discouragement or disengagement. Subsequent questions delve into increasingly higher-order involvement in the text. Students are asked why a passage is written the way it is and if they feel that the author's choices were ultimately successful. This type of instruction and questioning not only makes students better readers, it also makes them better writers as they consider the decisions authors make and the effects those choices have on the text and the reader.

All About Annotation
Teacher Instructions

Annotation is the practice of making notes on a text during reading, and it is a crucial component of the close-reading process. It allows students to more deeply dissect a text and make note of the parts that intrigue or excite them, as well as the parts that confuse or disengage them. Annotation gives students a tool with which to interact with the text on their terms and in ways specific to their needs and interests.

Tips and Strategies

☑ This resource has been designed to give your students the space needed to annotate the reading passages. Extra space has been included in the margin to the left of the passage. In addition, room has also been added between each line of text, with even more space included between paragraphs.

☑ Share the student sample (page 7) to give your students an idea of what is expected of them and how annotation works. This sample only shows three basic ways of annotating: circling unfamiliar words, underlining main ideas, and writing key details. Begin with these to ensure that students understand the concept. Additional responsibilities and tasks can be added later.

☑ Much like the skill of summarization requires restraint, so does annotation. Give students a goal. For example, tell them they can only underline one main idea per paragraph and/ or their key notes for each paragraph can be no more than five words in length. If these expectations aren't given, students might make too many notes, circle too many words, and underline too much text. This would make the text more difficult to read and create the opposite effect of what is intended.

☑ If you see that a majority of your students are circling the same unfamiliar words and noting confusion in the same areas of the text, spend more time and focus on these parts.

☑ Instruct students to reference their annotations when answering more complex questions, such as those inquiring about the structural and inferential elements of the text.

☑ Annotations can be used as an assessment tool to determine how well students are analyzing a text or even how well they are following directions.

☑ If students need more room to annotate, consider allowing them to affix sticky notes onto their pages and add notes in this way.

☑ As students become more fluent at the skill of annotating, increase their responsibilities and/or add new tasks. Here are a few examples to consider:

  ♦ Add a question mark (?) for information they find confusing.

  ♦ Add an exclamation point (!) for information they find surprising.

  ♦ Draw arrows between ideas and/or elements to show connections.

  ♦ Keep track of characters' names and relationships.

  ♦ Add notes about such elements of authorial craft as tone, mood, or style.

All About Annotation (cont.)
Student Sample

> **Annotation** = making notes on a text as you read it

3 Basic Ways to Annotate a Text

Note key details.

In the left margin, write a few words that give key details from the paragraph. Your notes in this space should be brief. They should be five words or fewer.

Circle difficult words.

If you aren't sure what a word means, circle it. Once you determine its meaning, write the word's definition in the left margin and circle it.

Underline main ideas.

Find the main idea of each paragraph and underline it. The main idea gives the most important information the author is trying to tell you in that paragraph.

Flashlights Skyward

once a year

race
trails
mountains
100 miles

1 The Leadville Trail 100 Run ("Race Across the Sky") is an ultramarathon. It is a grueling test of strength, endurance, and mental will. Held annually in Leadville, Colorado, it takes place on trails and dirt roads in the heart of the Rocky Mountains. It is an out-and-back course. There is a time limit: runners have to go the 100-mile distance in under 30 hours.

high elevation makes runners sick

go up

2 Many runners start having problems before they even start running. This is because the race starts at an elevation of 9,020 feet. As there is less oxygen in the air at this elevation, one can suffer from altitude sickness if one has not trained or had time to get used to the height. During the race, runners will ascend peaks as high as 12,620 feet.

Flashlights Skyward

 The Leadville Trail 100 Run ("Race Across the Sky") is an ultramarathon. It is a grueling test of strength, endurance, and mental will. Held annually in Leadville, Colorado, it takes place on trails and dirt roads in the heart of the Rocky Mountains. It is an out-and-back course. There is a time limit: runners have to go the 100-mile distance in under 30 hours.

 Many runners start having problems before they even start running. This is because the race starts at an elevation of 9,020 feet. As there is less oxygen in the air at this elevation, one can suffer from altitude sickness if one has not trained or had time to get used to the height. During the race, runners will ascend peaks as high as 12,620 feet.

 An American wilderness guide brought a new and unusual team to the race in 1992. They were Tarahumara runners from Mexico. They dressed in their traditional skirts and capes and wore handmade sandals on their feet. The Tarahumara dropped out before the halfway point. The problem wasn't what they were wearing or their ability. It was the culture shock. The Tarahumara still lived a traditional life. They were not familiar with modern ways. For example, they had never seen a flashlight before. When they held these strange "torches," they pointed them skyward. At the aid stations, they didn't take food. They waited shyly to be offered it.

 The Tarahumara returned in 1993 and 1994. They raced only because they were offered corn for their villages. Each time, they wore their traditional skirts and capes. In 1994, they were given expensive, brand-name shoes to wear. The Tarahumara wore them until the first check-in station. Once there, they tore the shoes off their feet and threw them away. They continued on only after lacing up their traditional sandals.

5 The Tarahumara raced through snow and mud. They won easily both years. They set course records. One record of 17 hours and 30 minutes stood for eight years. What people noticed more than their clothes was that the Tarahumara never looked tired. While running, they just looked happy.

Your Name: _____   Partner: _____

Flashlights Skyward *(cont.)*

(**First**) Silently read "Flashlights Skyward." You might see words you do not know and read parts you do not understand. Keep reading! Determine what the story is mainly about.

(**Then**) Sum up the story. Write the main idea and most important information. If someone reads your summary, that person should know it is this story that you are writing about.

_____

_____

_____

_____

_____

_____

(**After That**) Read the story again. Use a pencil to circle or mark words you don't know. Note places that confuse you. Underline the main action or idea of each paragraph.

(**Next**) Meet with your partner. Help each other find these words in the text.

grueling   endurance   annually   elevation   ascend

Read the sentences around the words. Think about how they fit in the whole story. Think about what the words must mean. Then mark each sentence as **T** (True) or **F** (False). On the lines provided, write the information in the story that helped you answer.

___F___ **a.** When something is **grueling**, it is easy. It says the Leadville 100 is a grueling

race. Any race that's 100 miles is not easy!

_____ **b.** If one has lots of **endurance**, one has lots of staying power and can keep going.

_____

_____ **c.** If something happens **annually**, it happens once every 10 years.

_____

_____ **d.** If you're at a high **elevation**, you are at a low altitude. _____

_____

_____ **e.** If you **ascend** a mountain, you go up it. _____

_____

Your Name: _____

Flashlights Skyward (cont.)

(Now)   Answer the story questions below.

1. What happened to the Tarahumara runners the first time they raced? _____

_____

Why did it happen? Give specific details from the story that supports your answer.

_____

_____

2. You are told the Leadville 100 is an "out-and back-course." For how many miles do runners have to retrace their steps? Explain how you got your answer.

_____

_____

3. You are told in the first paragraph that the race takes place "in the heart of" the Rocky Mountains. What does the author mean by this phrase?

_____

What information in the story helps you know what it is like in the heart of these mountains?

_____

_____

4. Draw a picture to answer the questions posed in each box below.

What type of footwear did the Tarahumara runners wear at the beginning of the 1994 race?	What type of footwear did the Tarahumara runners wear at the end of the 1994 race?

Why do your pictures show different shoes? Quote part of the story in your answer.

_____

_____

Your Name: _____

Flashlights Skyward (cont.)

Then Reread the entire story one last time. Think about how the story can be divided into two parts.

5. In just one sentence, tell what paragraphs 1 and 2 are mainly about.

_____

In just one sentence, tell what paragraphs 3–5 are mainly about.

_____

6. Why do you think the author presented the information in the paragraph order that she did?

_____

_____

What do you think the author might have wanted you to think about after you were done reading?

_____

_____

7. Why do you think the Tarahumara did better the second and third time they entered the race? Use details from the story in your answer.

_____

_____

_____

Think of a time or experience where you did better the second or third time you tried. Tell why you think you did so.

_____

_____

_____

 Learn More Use books or the Internet to research ultramarathons (the Leadville 100 or a different one) or the Tarahumara. On the back of this paper, write five pieces of information about your chosen topic.

Mystery Solved

1 Ava and Ethan wanted to solve mysteries. They wanted to follow in their father's footsteps and become detectives. Their father had advised them to read on a variety of subjects. "Reading will give you a solid foundation for any field," he said. "Reading is a window to the world. It is like a garden carried in your pocket. Yes, with reading as your base, you will be well prepared for detective work or any other kind of career."

2 Ada and Ethan read fiction and nonfiction. They also enjoyed reading to each other or listening to books on tape. One day, they were sitting and reading in the school library when Brenda came up to them. "Summer has my five dollar bill!" she cried. "She insists that she found it between pages 35 and 36 in the book she's reading. I don't care how staunchly she says it's hers, I know it's mine. I set it down on the table just for a second."

3 Ethan said, "Summer didn't find it between pages 35 and 36. I know, because all books are printed with the odd-numbered pages on the right. Therefore, pages 35 and 36 are the front and back of a single page, and nothing could have been found between them."

4 A few weeks later Ada and Ethan went on a field trip to the art museum. The docent who was the volunteer guide for that day said, "This painting is from the early 14th century. It depicts a typical scene from a country kitchen in France. You can see the woman is kneading bread. Onions are hanging from the wall, and there are potatoes and tomatoes in baskets against the wall. The artist is very famous. You can see his signature if you look closely at the right corner."

5 Ada gazed intently at the canvas. Then she said, "This painting is a forgery. It's fake." When the docent said she didn't know how a little school child could know, Ada said, "I may not know about art, but I can read. I read one book about food origins, or where they came from. Potatoes and tomatoes came from the Americas. France is in Europe. Potatoes and tomatoes weren't brought to Europe until the late 15th century."

Your Name: _____   Partner: _____

Mystery Solved (cont.)

First   Silently read "Mystery Solved." You might see words you do not know and read parts you do not understand. Keep reading! Determine what the story is mainly about.

Then   Sum up the story. Write the main idea and most important information. If someone reads your summary, that person should know it is this story that you are writing about, not a different story!

_____

_____

_____

_____

_____

_____

After That   Read the story again. Use a pencil to circle or mark words you don't know. Note places that confuse you. Underline the main action or idea of each paragraph.

Next   Meet with your partner. Help each other find these words in the text.

foundation   staunchly   docent   volunteer   forgery   origins

Read the sentences around the words. Think about how they fit in the whole story. Think about what the words mean and then tell how the story gives you the following information. The first one has been done for you.

a. A **foundation** is a starting point or base. <u>Their father says "reading will give them</u>

<u>a solid foundation" and "with reading as their base, they are well prepared."</u>

b. A **staunch** reply is said firmly and strongly. _____

_____

c. A **docent** is not a paid worker. _____

_____

d. A **forgery** is not the real thing. _____

_____

e. A person's **origins** is where he/she is from. _____

_____

Your Name: _____

Mystery Solved *(cont.)*

Now   Answer the story questions below.

1. Why did Ada know the painting was a forgery when she saw the potatoes and tomatoes in it?

_____

_____

_____

_____

2. If you open up a book, will the page number on the left-hand side by even or odd?

_____

Quote one sentence of Ethan's that helps you know your answer above is correct.

_____

_____

3. In paragraph 1, Ada and Ethan's father describes reading as a "window to the world" and "a garden carried in your pocket." Pick one of those phrases and explain what he means.

_____

_____

_____

Which parts of the story help you know you are right?

_____

_____

_____

4. What hint is there in the story that it was usual for people in France in the 14th century to make their own bread?

_____

_____

_____

_____

Your Name: _____

Mystery Solved (cont.)

Then Reread the entire story one last time. Think about the author's purpose for writing the story as you read.

5. In paragraph 1, what is the main message you are given about reading?

_____

_____

How is that message reinforced in the rest of the story?

_____

_____

6. Do you think the author did a good job showing the importance of reading? Explain.

_____

_____

_____

Can you think of another example or time in your life when reading or having read something helped you know what to do?

_____

_____

_____

7. You are told that the painting depicts a typical scene from a country kitchen in France. An action is described, as well as some details. Use this as a model to write a few sentences that describe a typical scene in the kitchen in your home. Make sure you include at least one action and two details.

_____

_____

_____

_____

Learn More Research the origins of other foods. On the back of this paper, write a short paragraph in which a mystery is solved by someone because that person knows a particular food origin.

New Flag Needed!

1 In 1936 Liechtenstein competed at the Summer Olympics for the first time. Immediately afterward, Liechtenstein decided to change its national flag. This was done because of what was seen at the Opening Ceremony. In 1936, 50 nations took part in this event. One of those was Haiti. During the Opening Ceremony, everyone could see that Haiti's flag was evenly divided into two horizontal stripes. The top half of Haiti's flag was blue, and the bottom half was red. It looked exactly like Liechtenstein's flag. The two flags were identical! In 1937, Liechtenstein changed its flag by adding a gold crown in the top left corner. Haiti chose to retain its design until 1964.

2 National flags are used to identify a country. Some stand out. For example, Switzerland's flag stands out because it is one of only two square flags. (The Vatican has the only other square flag.) It also stands out because it is not always square! Confused? When the Swiss flag is displayed on ships and at sea, it cannot be square. It must be wider than it is tall. When it is displayed on land, it is almost always square. No matter its shape, the Swiss flag is always red with a white cross in the center.

3 While only two countries have square flags, only one country has a flag that isn't a rectangle. (Did you know that all squares are rectangles, but not all rectangles are squares?) Only Nepal's flag is not rectangular. Nepal is home to eight of the world's ten tallest mountains, and its flag consists of two triangles. These triangles represent the peaks of the Himalayan Mountains.

 4 A quick glance seems to show that the flags of Monaco and Indonesia are as alike as two peas in a pod. They both have two equal horizontal bands. The top stripe is red, and the bottom stripe is white. Yet, a close examination shows that the flags are a tad different. Monaco's is slightly narrower.

 5 One may also be tricked by the flags of Republic of Ireland and Ivory Coast. These are identical tricolor flags, except the order of colors is reversed. From the left to right, the bars for Ireland are green, white, and orange. From the left to right, Ivory Coast's three bars are orange, white, and green.

Your Name: _____ Partner: _____

New Flag Needed! (cont.)

First Silently read "New Flag Needed!" You might see words you do not know and read parts you do not understand. Keep reading! Determine what the story is mainly about.

Then Sum up the story. Write down the main idea and most important information. If someone reads your summary, that person should know it is this story that you are writing about, not a different story!

_____

_____

_____

_____

_____

After That Read the story again. Use a pencil to circle or mark words you don't know. Note places that confuse you. Underline the main action or idea of each paragraph.

Next Meet with your partner. Help each other find these new words in the text.

horizontal   represent   displayed   retained   tricolor

Read the sentences around the words. Think about how they fit in the whole story. Define the words. Which information from the text helped you figure out the meaning of the words? An example is given for you.

Word	Definition	Information That Helps
horizontal		
represent	to stand for something	The triangles stand for the peaks of the mountains.
displayed		
retain		
tricolor		

Your Name: _____

New Flag Needed! (cont.)

Now   Answer the story questions below.

1. Why did Liechtenstein add a gold crown to its flag after the 1936 Olympic Games?

_____

_____

On what color was the gold crown added? Check the correct box.   ❑ blue   ❑ red

Explain how the story helped you know this answer.

_____

_____

2. In the box below, draw a ship that is flying a Swiss flag. On the lines to the right, explain why you drew the flag the way you did. Explain both its shape and its design.

_____

_____

_____

_____

3. In paragraph 4, the phrase "as alike as two peas in a pod" is used in the first sentence. What does this saying mean in the way it is used here?

_____

How did the story help you know? _____

_____

4. Use the spaces below to draw two flags. Look at the labels to see which flags to draw. For each flag, write in words to show which colors go where.

Republic of Ireland   **Ivory Coast**

Your Name: _____

New Flag Needed! *(cont.)*

Then Reread the entire story one last time. As you read, think about the main idea of each paragraph.

5. The title of the story fits best with the main idea of paragraph 1. Write a title for each of the other paragraphs. Each title should sum up the main idea of just that paragraph.

Paragraph 1: _New Flag Needed!_____

Paragraph 2: _____

Paragraph 3: _____

Paragraph 4: _____

Paragraph 5: _____

6. Go back and read the descriptions of the flags. As you read, use the words to make a picture in your head of each flag. Close your eyes for a second and visualize the flags.

 a. Which flag was the easiest to picture? _____

 Why? _____

 _____

 b. Which flag was the most difficult to picture? _____

 Why? _____

 _____

7. Imagine you go to a party and find that someone is dressed the same as you. Do you think you would feel the same as the people from Liechtenstein felt when they found out Haiti had the same flag? Tell why or why not. (You cannot be wrong because it's your opinion, but you must defend your answer.)

_____

_____

_____

Learn More You may have never heard of some of the countries mentioned in the story. Pick one country, and learn about it. Describe in complete sentences where the country is located and what language most of its citizens speak.

Garrulous Gabby

 Gabriela had a nickname that she despised. Every time she heard it, she would feel her blood boil. "I hate it!" she complained angrily to her mother. "I don't mind being called 'Gabby': it has a wonderful and happy ring to it. I despise being called 'garrulous,' however. I never get to finish a story. After about 20 minutes when I still have over a million words left, my classmates will say, 'Garrulous Gabby, Garrulous Gabby, that's enough!' Mother, I'm telling you that my classmates are just plain mean!"

 Gabriela took a deep breath, as she intended to continue, but her mother seized that tiny silver of silence to speak. "Darling," she said, firmly but gently, "You need to learn to listen. A conversation is carried on between two people. It can't be one-sided."

 "But I never get to finish my side of the conversation!" Gabriela protested. "Even before I'm close to finishing, when I still have over a million words left, they interrupt me to say, 'Garrulous Gabby, that's enough!'"

 Gabriela would have continued, but her mother shushed her. "Don't let my advice fall on deaf ears," she said. At that point, Gabriela started to talk about ears. She talked about how polar bears have little ones so they won't freeze. She talked about how elephants have big, thin ones with lots of veins running through them. She explained that this made their ears like air conditioners. She said this was because when the elephants flapped their ears, it cooled all the blood running through the veins.

5 The next day at school, Gabriela's teacher said everyone had to write a story for a citywide contest. Gabriela started to speak, but her teacher said, "Talk with the written word. Use your words to make pictures." Gabriela spent a long time on her story. She described a lonely girl who talked too much but eventually learned to listen to others and made friends. Gabriela was shocked to hear that she had won. After her story was read aloud, her classmates asked Gabriela to tell them how she felt. She opened her mouth, but nothing came out. Gabriela wasn't garrulous. She was speechless!

Your Name: _____ Partner: _____

Garrulous Gabby *(cont.)*

First Silently read "Garrulous Gabby." You might see words you do not know and read parts you do not understand. Keep reading! Determine what the story is mainly about.

Then Sum up the story. Write the main idea and most important information. If someone reads your summary, that person should know it is this story that you are writing about, not a different story!

_____

_____

_____

_____

_____

_____

After That Read the story again. Use a pencil to circle or mark words you don't know. Note places that confuse you. Underline the main action or idea of each paragraph.

Next Meet with your partner. Help each other find these new words in the text.

despised   garrulous   seized   advice

Read the sentences around the words. Think about how they fit in the whole story. Think about what the words must mean. Then mark each sentence as **T** (True) or **F** (False). Tell what information in the story helped you and your partner know.

_____ **a.** When you **despise** something, you really like it. _____

_____

_____

_____ **b.** Someone who is **garrulous** talks a lot. _____

_____

_____ **c.** When you **seize** something, you ignore it. _____

_____

_____ **d.** When you give **advice**, you give information that helps guide someone.

_____

_____

Your Name: _____

Garrulous Gabby (cont.)

Now   Answer the story questions below.

1. Which part of Gabriela's nickname does she like? _____

Why does she like it? _____

_____

2. Gabriela's mother gives Gabriela some advice. Does it fall on deaf ears? Explain using details from the beginning and the end of the story.

_____

_____

_____

3. In the story, it says that Gabriela "would feel her blood boil." What is meant by this expression?

_____

Which parts of the story help you know you are right?

_____

_____

4. Explain how an elephant's ears help keep it cool.

_____

_____

_____

Do you think Gabriela was right to compare an elephant's ears to an air conditioner? Tell why or why not.

_____

_____

_____

Your Name: _____

Garrulous Gabby *(cont.)*

Then   Reread the entire story one last time.

5. Think about how the word *garrulous* is used throughout the story.

     a. What is the part of speech of the word *garrulous* as it is used in Gabriela's nickname? Check one box and explain why it is this part of speech.

         ❑ noun   ❑ verb   ❑ adjective   ❑ pronoun

         _____

         _____

     b. Does the author ever give you the definition of the word *garrulous*? _____

     c. The word *garrulous* means "talkative and chatty, especially about matters that aren't important." How does the author *show* you this definition?

         _____

         _____

6. The author may have written this story to help you increase your vocabulary, but it was not her main reason. What big lesson do you think the author wanted you to learn? You may want to quote some words from the story as part of your answer.

_____

_____

7. The teacher tells Gabriela to "Talk with the written word. Use your words to make pictures." Pick an object you can see in your classroom. Do not name it, but describe it. Write at least four sentences. One of your sentences should start like this: "It is like. . . ."

_____

_____

_____

_____

 Learn More   The ears of polar bears and elephants are mentioned in the story. Now research hippopotamus ears. Where are they located and why? What's special about them?

Knocked Flat

1   Should children be shielded? Should they only hear stories where everything comes up roses? Should they be protected from tales of horrible deeds and misfortune? The poet Hilaire Belloc didn't think so. Although Belloc wrote humorous verse, his poems were not about cheerful children throwing snowballs or spotting robins nesting in cherry trees. Belloc's poems were cautionary tales. They served as warnings. In a funny way, they informed children what dire consequences would befall them if they didn't behave.

2   One of Belloc's poems is about a girl named Rebecca who practiced "A trick that everyone abhors." What did she do that everyone hated: she slammed doors. Her door-slamming ended when a marble statue fell on her. The marble statue was "Above the door this little lamb / Had carefully prepared to slam, / And down it came! It knocked her flat! / It laid her out! She looked like that."

3   Belloc makes sure you have no doubts about the dire consequences that befell Rebecca because the next verse is all about her funeral. One is told that the sermon ". . . showed the dreadful end of one / Who goes and slams the door for fun."

4   Belloc was born on July 27 in 1870. He died on July 16, 1953. Belloc's father was French, but his mother was English. Although born in France, Belloc spent most of his life in England. Belloc was a prolific writer. When people asked him why he wrote so much, he replied, "because my children are howling for pearls and caviar."

5   The poem about Rebeccaa can be found in Belloc's well-known *Cautionary Tales for Children*, which also contains a poem about "Jim, who ran away from his nurse, and was eaten by a lion." Other tales are about "Matilda, who told lies and was burnt to death," and "Sarah Byng, who could not read and was tossed into a thorny hedge by a bull." The jury is out when it comes to what children should be protected from, but perhaps what we can learn from Belloc is that when it comes to lessons, humor can't hurt.

Your Name: _____ Partner: _____

Knocked Flat *(cont.)*

First Silently read "Knocked Flat." You might see words you do not know and read parts you do not understand. Keep reading! Determine what the story is mainly about.

Then Sum up the story. Write the main idea and most important information. If someone reads your summary, that person should know it is this story that you are writing about.

_____

_____

_____

_____

_____

_____

After That Read the story again. Use a pencil to circle or mark words you don't know. Note places that confuse you. Underline the main action or idea of each paragraph.

Next Meet with your partner. Help each other find these new words in the text.

deeds   dire   consequences   abhors   prolific

Read the sentences around the words. Think about how they fit in the whole story. Define the words. Which information from the text helped you figure out the meaning of the words?

Word	Definition	Information That Helps
deeds		
dire		
consequences		
abhors		
prolific		

Your Name: _____

Knocked Flat *(cont.)*

Now   Answer the story questions below.

1. What happens to Rebecca and why? _____

_____

2. Does Belloc think reading is important? Use evidence and/or a quote from the passage to defend your answer.

_____

_____

_____

3. In the first paragraph, there is a sentence that contains the phrase "everything comes up roses." What is meant by this expression?

_____

How do you know? Which parts of the story helped you answer?

_____

_____

4. In the story, we are told what Belloc says when he is asked why he writes so much. Fill out the form below to examine what he says.

His quote: _____

_____

What this quote means: _____

_____

Why does he use these two examples of things his children want? What do these things represent?

_____

_____

_____

_____

Your Name: _____

Knocked Flat *(cont.)*

Then Reread the entire story one last time. As you read, think about the question asked at the beginning of the story and how the author answers it.

5. Why do you think the author starts the story with a question?

_____

_____

Try reading the story again, but this time start on the 5th sentence in paragraph 1. If you start there, does the story have the same effect? Is your attention captured? Tell why or why not.

_____

_____

_____

6. Does the author actually answer the question asked at the beginning of the story? Defend and explain your answer with words or evidence from the text.

_____

_____

_____

7. What does the author feel the reader should have learned from Belloc when it comes to lessons?

_____

_____

Do you agree? Use an example from your own life to support your answer.

_____

_____

Learn More Find the complete text of some of Belloc's stories from *Cautionary Tales for Children.* (They are available for free online if your library does not have a copy of the book.) Select one poem, and then write a paragraph in which you explain whether or not you think a child should be shielded from that particular poem. Use the back of this paper.

Hard to Believe

1   Having put their children to bed, Mr. and Mrs. Martinez leaned back on the couch and put their feet up. They were set to enjoy their grown-up time, when they heard wild laughter coming from their children's room. Mr. and Mrs. Martinez stormed into the room. "We're really irate," they cried, "and we're getting angrier by the second. You know it's time to go to sleep! This is our time to relax! Now be quiet, close your eyes, and go to sleep!"

2   "It was the hyena under the bed," the children protested. "He's the culprit! He's the one who is doing all the wild laughing. You shouldn't be mad at us. We're innocent! We've done nothing wrong!"

3   "That's enough!" the parents yelled before closing the door tightly behind them and heading back down the stairs. They hadn't gone more than halfway down when the wild laughing started again. Immediately, they retraced their steps and swung the door open. "You've been warned!" they said, their voices shaking in fury. "Once more, and you will be punished!"

4   Despite the warnings, there was wild laughter from the room two more times. As they made their way back to the couch, Mr. Martinez said wearily, "I'm tired of their lying. They keep saying they're innocent victims, and they blame a hyena under the bed. I've never heard of anything so ridiculous. I don't know which makes me angrier: that we've ordered them to stop and they won't, or that they think we would believe such a ridiculous story."

5   Mr. Martinez stopped talking only when he bumped into Mrs. Martinez. She had stopped suddenly on the bottom step. Funny sounds were coming out of her mouth while she raised a shaking hand and pointed to the couch. There, making itself comfortable, was a crocodile. "I know what would make me the most irate," the crocodile said as it rearranged cushions. "It's ridiculous that your children expect you to believe their silly story about a hyena laughing while under the bed. Why would a hyena be under the bed when it could be on top of the bed? No animal would take a hard, cold floor over a soft, cozy piece of furniture."

Your Name: _____   Partner: _____

Hard to Believe (cont.)

First Silently read "Hard to Believe." You might see words you do not know and read parts you do not understand. Keep reading! Determine what the story is mainly about.

Then Sum up the story. Write the main idea and most important information. If someone reads your summary, that person should know it is this story that you are writing about, not a different story!

_____

_____

_____

_____

_____

After That Read the story again. Use a pencil to circle or mark words you don't know. Note places that confuse you. Underline the main action or idea of each paragraph.

Next Meet with your partner. Help each other find these new words in the text.

irate   culprit   innocent   wearily   ridiculous

Read the sentences around the words. Think about how they fit in the whole story. Then match the words to their synonyms. Tell which part of the story helped you know you were right.

  a. "not guilty" = _____ I know, because in the story,

  _____

  b. "silly" = _____ I know, because in the story,

  _____

  c. "wrongdoer" = _____culprit_____ I know, because in the story, _the children say_

  they are innocent and the hyena is the culprit, or one who is laughing.

  d. "tiredly" = _____ I know, because in the story,

  _____

  e. "mad" = _____ I know, because in the story,

  _____

Your Name: _____

Hard to Believe (cont.)

Now) Answer the story questions below.

1. Why did Mr. and Mrs. Martinez go into the children's room? _____

_____

2. Why didn't Mr. and Mrs. Martinez look for the hyena under the bed?

_____

_____

3. In paragraph 1, you are told that Mr. and Mrs. Martinez "stormed into the room." What does this expression mean in the way it is used here?

_____

_____

How does the story help you know this information?

_____

_____

4. In paragraph 5, Mrs. Martinez sees something. In the box below, draw a picture of what she sees. On the lines, write a few words that describe how she felt when she saw this.

_____

_____

_____

_____

How did you know what Mrs. Martinez was feeling when she saw this? Tell which parts of the story gave you this information.

_____

_____

_____

Your Name: _____

Hard to Believe (cont.)

Then   Reread the entire story one last time. As you read, think about how the last paragraph relates to the rest of the passage.

5. Do you think the children were ever punished? Tell why or why not. (Your answer cannot be wrong because it is your opinion, but you must defend your answer.)

_____

_____

Would your answer have been the same if you had only read the first four paragraphs? Tell why or why not.

_____

_____

6. Fiction can be realistic. Is this story realistic? Tell why or why not.

_____

_____

_____

7. The story might have had a very different ending if Mr. and Mrs. Martinez had looked under the bed immediately after the children told them a hyena was under it.

Imagine you are the author. You are just beginning paragraph 3, and one of the parents is going to be looking under the bed. Write the first four lines of the paragraph.

_____

_____

_____

_____

_____

_____

 Learn More   Do hyenas really laugh? Look in books or online to find out.

Movie-Watching Locusts

1   Locusts are some of the most destructive insects on the planet. In the solitary phase, these short-horned grasshoppers are harmless. One locust can't do much damage. This all changes when locusts swarm. Large swarms can consist of billions of insects. Some swarms are so huge that when the locusts take flight, they darken the sky for days. The air roars with the sound of their wings. When they land, they consume everything. They will eat every bit of green in minutes. Nothing is left but bare ground.

2   Scientists have studied why locusts swarm. One scientist did something else with these destructive insects. The scientist's name was Dr. Claire Rind, a biologist and a robotics expert. Rind made the locusts watch a movie. She made them watch *Star Wars*.

3   Rind wanted to design a collision-avoidance system for cars. She wanted to make cars that wouldn't crash into each other. Rind knew that locusts don't bump into each other, even when there are so many insects that the swarm blocks out the sun. Locusts have simple eyes and brains, and yet they avoid collisions. Rind wanted cars to be able to do what locusts do.

4   While the locusts watched *Star Wars*, Rind kept track of what was going on in their eyes and in their brains. She found out that locusts have special neurons that respond to objects moving at them. (A neuron is a special cell that carries messages between the brain and other parts of the body.) *Star Wars* was the perfect movie to have the locusts watch, because it contains several scenes where spaceships seem to fly toward the viewer, away from the viewer, and to the left and right of the viewer.

5   Once Rind understood how the locust's neural system worked, she made a robot. It had cameras for eyes, and its inner workings reacted in the same way the locusts' neural system did. Rind sent her robot zooming through an obstacle course. It did hit some obstacles, but the project was off to a great start. Thanks to movie-watching locusts, the robot was able to avoid collisions about nine out of ten times!

Your Name: _____ Partner: _____

Movie-Watching Locusts (cont.)

First Silently read "Movie-Watching Locusts." You might see words you do not know and read parts you do not understand. Keep reading! Determine what the story is mainly about.

Then Sum up only <u>paragraphs 2–5</u> of the story. Write the main idea and most important information. If someone reads your summary, that person should know it is this story that you are writing about, not a different story!

_____

_____

_____

_____

_____

After That Read the story again. Use a pencil to circle or mark words you don't know. Note places that confuse you. Underline the main action or idea of each paragraph.

Next Meet with your partner. Help each other find these new words in the text.

solitary   swarm   consume   collision   obstacle

Read the sentences around the words. Think about how they fit in the whole story. Discuss how the author helped you know what the words meant. Then pick one word each. Make sure you each choose a different word. Fill in the blanks.

a. My partner's word: _____

My partner thinks that in this passage the word must mean _____

_____

I agree because in the passage, _____

_____

b. My word: _____

I think that in this passage this word must mean _____

_____

My partner agrees because in the passage, _____

_____

Your Name: _____

Movie-Watching Locusts *(cont.)*

Now   Answer the story questions below.

1. What does Rind want to design? _____

_____

Why? _____

_____

_____

2. Why does the phrase "the air roars with the sound of their wings" help you understand how large a locust swarm can be?

_____

_____

_____

3. Which movie did Rind have locusts watch? _____

Why did Rind choose this movie? _____

_____

_____

_____

Can you think of another movie that would have worked just as well as this one? Name the movie, and explain your answer.

_____

_____

_____

4. Use the information given in the story to answer this question: Is the robot system that Rind made ready to be tested in cars? Why or why not? Defend your answer with evidence from the text.

_____

_____

_____

_____

Your Name: _____

Movie-Watching Locusts *(cont.)*

Then   Reread the entire story once more. Think about how paragraph 1 relates to the rest of the story.

5. What is paragraph 1 mainly about? Sum it up in two or three sentences.

_____

_____

_____

_____

6. Was paragraph 1 necessary for the rest of the passage to make sense? Explain.

_____

_____

_____

Why do you think the author included it? What do you think she hoped that readers would take from it?

_____

_____

_____

7. Imagine you are the one writing the story about locusts watching *Star Wars*. Using information from the story you just read, write the first two lines of the "newer and better" story. Make it exciting. Hook your reader into wanting more!

_____

_____

_____

_____

_____

 Learn More   Find out more about locusts by looking in books or online. On the back of this paper, write one paragraph discussing what you have learned. Your paragraph should have at least five facts.

Mind Reading

 Josie (*smugly*): I can read your mind! Choose a number between 1 and 10. Then multiply it by 9.

Cesar (*incredulously*): You can't read my mind! It's impossible, but I'll play along. Okay, I chose a number between 1 and 10, and I multiplied it by 9.

 Josie (*commandingly*): Now add the numbers or digits in your answer. Once you add them together, subtract 5 from your sum.

Cesar (*confidently*): A piece of cake! Done!

 Josie (*instructively*): Match that number to the corresponding letter in the alphabet. A = 1, B = 2, and so on. Then think of a country that begins with that letter.

Cesar (*impatiently*): Are we almost done? Okay, I matched my number to the corresponding letter in the alphabet, and I thought of a country.

 Josie (*firmly*): Now take the second letter of the country you thought of and think of an animal that starts with that letter.

Cesar (*peevishly*): Ugh, this is taking too long! Fine, I thought of an animal.

Josie (*jokingly*): Cesar! You know elephants are not native to Denmark!

Cesar (*astoundingly*): What? How did you do that? My country was Denmark, and my animal was an elephant!

 Josie (*laughingly*): If my instructions were followed correctly, you always come up with a "4." The corresponding letter in the alphabet is "D." There are only five countries that start with D. They are the Democratic Republic of Congo, Denmark, Dominica, Dominican Republic, and Djibouti. Most people will think of Denmark. There are lots of animals that start with an E, but most people will think of an elephant.

Cesar (*pensively*): After thinking this over, I bet that if I tried this trick in East Africa, most people would choose the country Djibouti.

Your Name: _____ Partner: _____

Mind Reading *(cont.)*

First   Silently read "Mind Reading." You might see words you do not know and read parts you do not understand. Keep reading! Determine what the play is mainly about.

Then   Sum up the play. Write the main idea and most important information. If someone reads your summary, that person should know it is this play that you are writing about.

_____

_____

_____

_____

_____

_____

_____

_____

_____

After That   Read the play again. Use a pencil to circle or mark words you don't know. Note places that confuse you. Underline the main action or idea of each paragraph.

Next   Meet with your partner. Look at all the words in parentheses that describe each character's tone of voice when he or she is speaking. Use what the characters say to help you and your partner define the words. Then write a phrase or a sentence you might say if you were speaking with the same tone of voice. The first one is done for you.

    a. smugly _"You can't fool me!"_ _____

    b. incredulously _____

    c. commandingly _____

    d. confidently _____

    e. impatiently _____

    f. peevishly _____

    g. astoundingly _____

    h. pensively _____

Your Name: _____

Mind Reading *(cont.)*

Now   Answer the questions below.

1. Why is Josie sure that Cesar will think of a country that begins with the letter D?

_____

_____

_____

_____

2. Imagine Cesar chose the number 5. Using numbers and mathematical symbols, write out the next three things he did.

Step 1: _Cesar chose the number 5._____

Step 2: _____

Step 3: _____

Step 4: _____

3. At one point, Cesar uses the expression "a piece of cake." What does he mean?

_____

How does the story help you know that you are right? _____

_____

_____

4. If Josie had asked Cesar to come up with an animal that was the last letter of the country he chose, what do you think is the most likely animal he would think of? Write it in the box.

```
┌ ─ ─ ─ ─ ─ ─ ─ ─ ─ ─ ─ ─ ─ ┐



└ ─ ─ ─ ─ ─ ─ ─ ─ ─ ─ ─ ─ ─ ┘
```

Why do you think so? _____

_____

_____

Your Name: _____

Mind Reading *(cont.)*

Then   Reread the entire play one last time. Think about all the steps Josie makes Cesar go through.

5. Write down Josie's Mind Reading trick as a "how-to". Number the steps. Include an example as part of each step.

Step	Instruction	Example
1		
2		
3		
4		
5		
6		

6. If you were going to teach someone how to do Josie's Mind Reading trick, would the play or your "how-to" be a better teaching tool? Explain your answer.

_____

_____

_____

7. Read the play out loud. Make your voices match the tone in parentheses. Then read the play out loud again, but this time without varying your voice. Which reading was better? Tell why.

_____

_____

_____

Learn More   Find the five countries that start with *D* on a map. Match the countries to these general areas: East Africa, Central Africa, Europe, and the Caribbean.

Principal's Office

 One of my favorite stories about being sent to the principal's office can be found in the book "Owls in the Family." The book was written by Farley Mowat. It is an autobiographical tale, and it focuses on a time in Mowat's childhood when he had two owls. Mowat had rescued the owls during the summer, and they had become his pets.

 When school started up, the first week did not go well. Mowat was tardy the first four days due to his avian pets. Mowat bicycled about two miles to school. The owls were used to following Mowat, so Mowat would have to turn around and take them back home. Mowat's father then told him to lock the owls in their pen before leaving. Mowat said the owls acted as if he had put them in jail. Wol, the larger of the two, was furious. He tore at the chicken wire with his beak and claws as Mowat rode away.

 Mowat raced off to school, but when he was almost there, he felt a huge rush of air as Wol landed on his shoulder. Mowat continued to pedal like mad, skidding into the schoolyard as the two-minute bell was ringing. Before rushing into the building, Mowat tied Wol to the bike's handlebars with a piece of twine.

4 Mowat had not done his homework, and the teacher had called him up to her desk to scold him. Mowat was wishing that the floor would open up and swallow him when suddenly there was a loud whump-whump-whump at the window. It was Wol! Being tied up had done nothing to discourage him. Wol was not one to let a little piece of string deter him. Wasting no time, Wol ducked through an open window and flew straight at Mowat.

5 Most likely, Wol meant to land on Mowat's shoulder, but he missed. Wol landed on the teacher's desk. The desk was polished hardwood, and unable to get a grip, Wol skated straight across the desk! Papers flew and books scattered all over the floor! Wol didn't stop until he landed plump in the middle of the teacher's lap! Mowat was sent to the principal's office, and the teacher went home for the rest of the day.

Your Name: _____ Partner: _____

Principal's Office (cont.)

First Silently read "Principal's Office." You might see words you do not know and read parts you do not understand. Keep reading! Determine what the story is mainly about.

Then Sum up the story. Write the main idea and most important information. If someone reads your summary, that person should know it is this story that you are writing about.

_____

_____

_____

_____

_____

_____

After That Read the story again. Use a pencil to circle or mark words you don't know. Note places that confuse you. Underline the main action or idea of each paragraph.

Next Meet with your partner. Help each other find these new words in the text.

avian   furious   twine   deter   scattered

Read the sentences around the words. Think about how they fit in the whole story. Then match the words to their synonyms. Tell which part of the story helped you and your partner know you were right.

Choose from these synonyms: *string, mad, strewn, bird, discourage*

a. avian = _____ We know because _____

_____

b. furious = _____ We know because _____

_____

c. twine = _____ We know because _____

_____

d. deter = _____ We know because _____

_____

e. scattered = _____ We know because _____

_____

Your Name: _____

Principal's Office *(cont.)*

Now   Answer the story questions below.

1. Who wrote the book "Owls in the Family"? _____

Why is "Owls in the Family" an autobiographical tale? _____

_____

_____

2. You are not told that Mowat was tardy on his fifth day of school, but use evidence from the story to tell why he might have been late.

_____

_____

_____

_____

3. In paragraph 3, you are told that Mowat continued to "pedal like mad." What is meant by this expression the way it is used here?

_____

_____

Which part of the story helped you know? _____

_____

_____

4. Would you describe Wol as wild or tame? You cannot be wrong because this is an opinion question, but you must defend your answer with evidence from the story.

_____

_____

_____

_____

_____

Your Name: _____

Principal's Office *(cont.)*

Then Reread the entire story one last time. As you read, think about what you expect after reading the title and what you know after reading just the first paragraph.

5. After reading just the title, what did you expect the story to be about?

_____

_____

After reading just paragraph 1, have your expectations changed? At that point, what do you expect to read about?

_____

_____

_____

6. How did the author create the action in the story of the morning on which Farley was sent to the principal's office? Give a few examples that help the reader picture the scene and understand what is happening in it.

_____

_____

_____

7. At one point in the story, Mowat wishes that the floor would open up and swallow him. Use your understanding of what Mowat meant to think of a time when you, someone you know, or a character in a book or movie felt this way. Tell what made you (or the person or character) feel this way.

_____

_____

_____

_____

Learn More Wol was a Great Horned Owl. Look in books or online to find out five facts about this bird. Write out your facts in paragraph from. One of your facts should be the bird's size and wingspan, as perhaps this will help you understand why the teacher went home.

Updated Fairy Tale

1   Once upon a time, Hannah and Greg lived happily at the edge of a forest. Hannah and Greg were twins, but they weren't identical twins. They didn't look exactly alike. They were fraternal twins. They lived with their parents and six other siblings. None of their other brothers or sisters was a twin. It was a happy life except for one thing: their other siblings were jealous that they weren't a twin.

2   One day, the other siblings decided to take Hannah and Greg deep into the forest and leave them there. The plan was to play hide and seek once they were in unfamiliar territory. When it was Hannah and Greg's turn to find them or seek them out, everyone else would band together and run home.

3   When they discovered they were alone, the twins tried to call home. Much to their dismay, their cell phones had no service. Then they remembered being taught to "hug a tree" if lost. This practice kept those who were lost from wandering in circles, and it meant that the rescuers' didn't have to retrace their steps and look again in places they had already searched. The twins decided to walk instead of follow the "hug a tree" lesson.

4   After hours and hours of walking in vain, they were spent. As well as tired and dirty, they were extremely hungry. Just when they were about to collapse, they saw a little cottage. The cottage had walls of gingerbread, a path made from hard candy, and window frames made of red licorice.

5   To their horror, a woman with nasty hairs coming out of her chin opened the door. The twins were terrified, but they soon learned the woman was an actress. The cottage was part of a movie set. Unbeknownst to them, Hannah and Greg had been filmed as they approached the cottage, and the director decided to make them part of the movie. He said the look of terror on their faces when the door opened was priceless. When the twins were dropped off at home, they never said a word about what had happened. They wanted to see the look of shock on their siblings' faces when they saw the twins on television. Only then could they live happily ever after.

Your Name: _____ Partner: _____

Updated Fairy Tale *(cont.)*

First   Silently read "Updated Fairy Tale." You might see words you do not know and read parts you do not understand. Keep reading! Determine what the story is mainly about.

Then   Sum up the story. Write the main idea and most important information. If someone reads your summary, that person should know it is this story that you are writing about, not a different story!

_____

_____

_____

_____

_____

_____

After That   Read the story again. Use a pencil to circle or mark words you don't know. Note places that confuse you. Underline the main action or idea of each paragraph.

Next   Meet with your partner. Help each other find these new words in the text.

      siblings   seek   dismay   vain   unbeknownst

Read the sentences around the words. Think about how they fit in the whole story. Think about what the words must mean. Then mark each sentence as **T** (True) or **F** (False). Tell what information in the story helped you and your partner know.

_____ **a.** A **sibling** can be a brother, but not a sister. <u>It says none of their other</u>

      <u>siblings was a twin, and they had both brothers and sisters.</u>

_____ **b.** When you **seek** something, you are looking for it. _____

      _____

_____ **c.** When one is **dismayed**, one is happy and content. _____

      _____

_____ **d.** If you look for something in **vain**, you find it easily. _____

      _____

_____ **e.** If something is **unbeknownst**, it isn't known. _____

      _____

Your Name: _____

Updated Fairy Tale (cont.)

Now   Answer the story questions below.

1. What type of twins are Hannah and Greg? _____

What type does the story say they are not? _____

How are the two types different? _____

_____

_____

2. Why should someone "hug a tree" if they are lost? Use evidence from the story.

_____

_____

_____

3. In paragraph 4, it says that the children are "spent." What is meant by this?

_____

_____

Which part of the story helped you know?

_____

_____

_____

4. Would you describe Hannah and Greg as patient? Use evidence from the story to do the following:

     a. Explain what the twins do to show that they are patient? _____

_____

_____

     b. Explain what the twins do to show that they are not very patient? _____

_____

_____

Your Name: _____

Updated Fairy Tale *(cont.)*

Then   Reread the entire story one last time. Think about what makes a fairy tale as you read.

5. You know this is a fairy tale from the title. What other words or phrases at the beginning and end helped you know?

Beginning: _____

End: _____

Why might someone who has not heard or read fairy tales have trouble with this question?

_____

_____

6. In a lot of fairy tales, there are evil or bad characters. Look at this line. Where on this scale would you place Hannah and Greg's siblings? Fill in a bubble to show your answer.

○——○——○——○——○——○——○——○

| Very Evil | | Very Good |

Now explain your answer. _____

_____

_____

7. Think of three other characters from fairy tales or any other fiction story. Write their names where they would belong on the scale above. Next, pick one of the characters you chose, and tell why you placed it to the left or right of Hannah and Greg's siblings.

_____

_____

_____

_____

Learn More   Find another version of *Hansel and Gretel* in a book or on the Internet. What version do you like better? Tell why, giving at least two specific examples of differences between the two versions.

Lung Capacity How-To

 It's time to blow out the candles. Some people can barely make the flame move or flicker. Other people can blow out every single candle with ease. It's time to go free diving, a sport where one dives as deeply as one can without any SCUBA gear or equipment. Some people can barely make it to the bottom of a backyard swimming pool. One expert in the sport was able to descend 830 feet into the watery depths!

 Our lungs are organs. (An organ is a group of tissues that perform a specific purpose or group of functions. One's heart, brain, liver, kidneys, and skin are organs, too.) The primary function of our lungs is to transport oxygen from the air we breathe into our bloodstream while taking away carbon dioxide. We release the carbon dioxide into the air when we breathe out. It is possible to increase the capacity or one's lungs. With regular exercise, it is possible to hold one's breath longer and take more air in.

 What is the current capacity of your lungs? How much air can your lungs take in right now? You can find out, but first you need to get a large bowl, a large plastic bottle with a lid, and a bendy straw. Once you have your materials, you fill the bowl about half full of water. Next, you fill the bottle with water. After putting the lid on it, you turn the bottle upside down in the bowl. Carefully remove the lid while you keep the spout under the water. The water will remain in the bottle because of the air pressure.

 The next thing to do is put the bendy part of the straw in the spout of the bottle. The final step is to blow into the straw as hard as you can! As the air from your lungs goes into the bottle, it will push the water in the bottle out. You can see what your lung capacity is by seeing how much air is in the bottle.

 It might be fun to try this again after doing 100 jumping jacks. Better yet, you could do this after a month of running every day. Your exercising might leave you with more air in the bottle. It might make it easy for you to blow out more than 100 candles or to free dive into the black depths of the ocean!

Your Name: _____   Partner: _____

Lung Capacity How-To (cont.)

First Silently read "Lung Capacity How-To." You might see words you do not know and read parts you do not understand. Keep reading! Determine what the story is mainly about.

Then Sum up the story. Write the main idea and most important information. If someone reads your summary, that person should know it is this story that you are writing about, not a different story!

_____

_____

_____

_____

_____

_____

After That Read the story again. Use a pencil to circle or mark words you don't know. Note places that confuse you. Underline the main action or idea of each paragraph.

Next Meet with your partner. Help each other find these new words in the text.

depths   primary   function   current   capacity

Read the sentences around the words. Think about how they fit in the whole story. Discuss how the author helped you know what the words meant. Then pick one word each. Make sure you each choose a different word. Fill in the blanks.

a. My partner's word: _____

My partner thinks that in this passage the word must mean _____

_____

I agree because in the passage _____

_____

b. My word: _____

I think that in this passage this word must mean _____

_____

My partner agrees because in the passage _____

_____

Your Name: _____

Lung Capacity How-To *(cont.)*

Now   Answer the story questions below.

1. According to the story, what is one reason why some people are able to blow out lots of candles on birthday cakes?

   _____

   _____

   _____

2. What is the lung's main function? Your answer should include the words *oxygen* and *carbon dioxide*?

   _____

   _____

   _____

   _____

3. Why is the kidney an organ? (Your answer cannot be because it says it is in the story, but you may quote words or a sentence from the story.)

   _____

   _____

   _____

4. How is SCUBA diving different from free diving?

   _____

   _____

   _____

   Which one would require a greater lung capacity? Why? _____

   _____

   _____

Your Name: _____

Lung Capacity How-To *(cont.)*

Then)   Reread the entire story one last time. Think about what makes this a good or poor how-to.

5. A "How-To" is a type of story that tells you how to do something. By this story's title, you can tell that it is meant to be a "How-To." What is the main thing the story is telling you how to do?

_____

In which of the story's paragraphs is this "how-to" information given? Check the boxes beside all the paragraphs that give this information.

❑ 1   ❑ 2   ❑ 3   ❑ 4   ❑ 5

6. Use the information from these paragraphs to write a better "How-To." Give it a title, list the materials, and show the steps in order. Only include information that is necessary.

Title: _____

Materials: _____

Step #1: _____

Step #2: _____

Step #3: _____

Step #4: _____

Step #5: _____

7. Think about the paragraphs that had nothing to do with the "How-To." What are those paragraphs mainly about?

_____

_____

What might be a better title for just those paragraphs? Why?

_____

_____

_____

Learn More   Using books or the Internet, find out five facts about another organ or the sport of free diving. On the back of this paper, write a title and then list your facts by number.

Stay Clear!

1   "You want to stay clear of that!" Maya shuddered. "This is all very scary. I don't know how it got here, but I know that I don't want to get any closer."

2   "It makes me want to tremble, too," Maya's partner Henry said. "It's a tree that would make anyone shake in fear." Henry took a step back and examined the Australian Gympie-Gympie from a safe distance. "Many botanists consider it to be one of the world's most dangerous trees," he said. "The entire plant is covered in hollow hairs that penetrate the skin on contact. The hairs deliver a potent neurotoxin. This poison is so powerful that the stinging sensation often lasts for two years! The pain is horrible. It's been described as being sprayed by burning acid. One botanist that studied this tree ended up in the hospital despite all her protective clothing!"

3   "Let's get out of here," Maya said, backing off. She turned and then gasped. "The nightmare continues," she cried, as she faced a giant hogweed plant. "That's another one to steer clear of. The sap of that plant causes blisters and long-lasting scars, and if it makes contact with our eyes, we'll go blind."

4   "Uh oh," Henry said eyeing a Himalayan Blackberry plant. "Look at the thorns on that monster! They're like one-inch shark teeth! You fall into those brambles, and you'd be slashed to pieces." Taking Maya's hand, he led her away from the blackberry plants. "Out of the frying pan into the fire," he muttered as the two of them were suddenly hit with a horrible smell.

5   "Skunk cabbage," Maya said. "It smells foul and disgusting, but at least it's not poisonous to touch. You can eat some parts of it, but others parts will make you really sick." Maya looked at Henry who was holding his nose, and she started to laugh. He looked at Maya as if she was crazy, but then he laughed, too. She said, "I was so disappointed when we didn't go to the zoo or the aquarium for our school field trip. I thought the botanical gardens would be boring. Wow, was I in for a surprise. All the information on the little signs is amazing, and who would think that we'd have to be separated from some plants by glass walls and hold our noses around others!"

Your Name: _____ Partner: _____

Stay Clear! *(cont.)*

First   Silently read "Stay Clear!" You might see words you do not know and read parts you do not understand. Keep reading! Determine what the story is mainly about.

Then   Sum up the story. Write the main idea and most important information. If someone reads your summary, that person should know it is this story that you are writing about, not a different story!

_____

_____

_____

_____

_____

_____

After That   Read the story again. Use a pencil to circle or mark words you don't know. Note places that confuse you. Underline the main action or idea of each paragraph.

Next   Meet with your partner. Help each other find these new words in the text.

     shuddered   tremble   botanists   potent   foul

Read the sentences around the words. Think about how they fit in the whole story. Define the words. Which information from the text helped you figure out the meaning of the words?

Word	Definition	Information That Helps
shuddered		
tremble		
botanist		
potent		
foul		

Your Name: _____

Stay Clear! (cont.)

Now Answer the story questions below.

1. Why would one want to stay away from the Australian Gympie-Gympie tree? Use evidence from the story in your answer. Write at least two sentences.

_____

_____

_____

_____

2. How does Henry compare the Himalayan blackberry plant to an animal?

_____

_____

What does he say would happen to you if you fell into the brambles? You may quote what Henry says for your answer.

_____

_____

3. In paragraph 4, Henry uses the expression "out of the frying pan and into the fire." What does this expression mean here?

_____

_____

What part of the story helps you know that you are right?

_____

_____

4. Do you think the skunk cabbage is surrounded by a glass wall? Use evidence from the story to defend your answer.

_____

_____

_____

_____

Your Name: _____

Stay Clear! *(cont.)*

Then   Reread the entire story one last time. Think about how you feel when you find out Maya and Henry are on a school field trip.

5. Imagine if paragraph 5 were missing. How would this change the story?

_____

_____

_____

_____

6. Why do you think the author made you wait for the end to find out Maya and Henry were visiting botanical gardens?

_____

_____

_____

Would you have liked the story better if you had known at the beginning that Maya and Henry were on a school field trip to the botanical gardens? Tell why or why not.

_____

_____

_____

_____

7. If you reread paragraphs 1 through 4 very carefully, you will find some subtle hints that Maya and Henry are not in the wild. Can you find one or more? (When something is subtle, it is clever and indirect.)

_____

_____

_____

_____

Learn More   Find out more about any of the plants mentioned or any other plant of your choice. On the back of this paper, write one paragraph about the plant. Include information about appearance, size, and what its native habitat is like.

Worth Billions

 Mars is the fourth planet in our solar system. It would take more than six of Mars to fill the volume of Earth. While Mars is a lot smaller than Earth, the two planets have about the same landmass. This is because around two-thirds of Earth's surface is covered in water. Mars also has a different surface gravity, which would allow you to leap nearly three times higher on Mars. If you weighed 100 pounds on Earth, you would weigh 38 pounds on Mars.

 While the previously stated facts are interesting, they serve only as an introduction to a question costing a pretty penny: Should we colonize Mars? It is a question worth hundreds of billions of dollars. Despite the astronomical price, I know the answer. The answer is yes. Yes, we should put a permanent colony on Mars. We need to push humankind to its limits. We need to boldly go where we've never been before.

 First, we have to think of survival of the species. I know some people think the money should go to helping people now, but that is shortsighted. We have to think beyond the next 100 years. As Stephen Hawkins, the famous scientist, said, "If the human race is to continue for another million years, we will have to boldly go where no one has gone before." We know for a fact that many species on our planet have already died out. If we had a colony on another planet, our species would survive even if Earth was destroyed or hit by a huge meteor.

 Second, we might detect life on Mars. We have currently sent rovers to Mars. These robots can't do what people can do. If life exists on Mars, it might be deep underground where there is water. People can dig much deeper and gather much more information than rovers.

 Finally, colonizing Mars will improve life on Earth. When scientists unite behind a common goal, research for one big idea helps in ways we can't even begin to imagine. For example, our space program worked to send people to the moon. As a result of this program, we now have microchips, scratch-resistant glasses, water filters, joysticks, cordless tools, and smoke detectors.

Your Name: _____ Partner: _____

Worth Billions *(cont.)*

First) Silently read "Worth Billions." You might see words you do not know and read parts you do not understand. Keep reading! Determine what the story is mainly about.

Then) Sum up <u>only paragraphs 2–5</u> of the story. Write the main idea and most important information of these paragraphs. If someone reads your summary, that person should know it is this story that you are writing about, not a different story!

_____

_____

_____

_____

_____

After That) Read the story again. Use a pencil to circle or mark words you don't know. Note places that confuse you. Underline the main action or idea of each paragraph.

Next) Meet with your partner. Help each other find these new words in the text.

colonize   astronomical   boldly   shortsighted   detect

Read the sentences around the words. Think about how they fit in the whole story. Define the words. Which information from the text helped you figure out the meaning of the words?

Word	Definition	Information That Helps
colonize		
astronomical		
boldly		
shortsighted		
detect		

Your Name: _____

Worth Billions (cont.)

(Now) Answer the story questions below.

1. Earth is not the same size as Mars. Is it bigger or smaller? _____

Why does Earth have the same landmass as Mars? _____

_____

2. How many main reasons did the author give for colonizing Mars? _____

Name them. _____

_____

_____

Which reason do you think is the strongest? Using at least one piece of evidence or fact from
the story, tell why. (You cannot be wrong, it is your opinion.)

_____

_____

3. Paragraph 1 includes the phrase "costing a pretty penny." What does this mean?

_____

What part of the story helped you know? _____

_____

4. The story names some common items that were invented as a result of our trips to the moon.
Choose two. Complete the chart by naming the items, drawing pictures of them, and thinking
about why they might have been useful to the space program.

Item	Drawing	Why Useful?

Your Name: _____

Worth Billions (cont.)

Then Reread the entire story one last time. Think about how paragraph 1 relates to the rest of the passage.

5. What is paragraph 1 mainly about? What is its purpose?

_____

_____

_____

6. After the introduction, the writer asks a rhetorical question. A rhetorical question is a question that is asked to make a point. The person who asks the question does not expect you to answer it. The person asking will answer it himself or herself. If he or she doesn't answer it, that's because the answer is obvious. What rhetorical question did the writer ask?

_____

Was the answer the author gives a fact or an opinion? _____

How do you know? _____

_____

_____

7. Over 200,000 people volunteered to go on a one-way trip to Mars. (It is one-way because of the length of the journey and because we don't have the technology to fuel a return trip.) Write out this rhetorical question: "Will I volunteer to go on a one-way trip to Mars?" Then answer it and tell why.

_____

_____

_____

_____

_____

Learn More Find out more information about Mars or another planet by looking in books or online. On the back of this paper, write down at least five pieces of information in paragraph form.

Superpower

1 "Your Majesty, I'm telling you it is true. I, too, thought the parents were exaggerating when they brought the child to me, but I now believe that he has a special gift. In fact, it's more than a gift. It's a superpower."

2 Her Majesty shook her head in denial. "The report is not credible," she said. "I don't believe it. I listened to it five times, and it is too incredible to be true." Seeing that her assistant was going to object, Her Majesty raised her hand. "Don't bother objecting," she said. "I know you're going to say that I should watch the performance, but I already did. I examined it thoroughly. It must be a trick. It's too incredible to be credible."

3 Her Majesty adjusted the earbud that was attached to her right ear. Most citizens had their earbuds attached to their left ears, but Her Majesty's right earbud signified that she had access to restricted information. Only government officials were allowed right earbuds. Government officials had left earbuds, too, but left earbuds were for personal use. People could listen to books, news, and send messages. Audio transmission was what connected the world. People kept their earbuds in at all times, because it was the only way they could communicate.

4 Her Majesty's assistant said, "We may be sitting on a goldmine with this child. His power is so valuable it is invaluable. It is so high, it cannot be calculated. Here he is. He is going to demonstrate his superpower to you." A shy boy slowly entered the room. He took his earbud out of his ear and put his personal communication device on the table. Her Majesty examined the boy closely to check that he was not secretly hooked to any device.

5 Her Majesty spoke to her own personal device and commanded it to show written words. Next, she slid her personal device over to the boy. Her Majesty's jaw dropped. She stared in amazement as she heard the boy read the words on her device. He stumbled over the letters at first, but his voice became stronger as he gained more confidence. "It's amazing!" Her Majesty cried. "He doesn't have to listen! He can read! He does have superpowers!"

Your Name: _____   Partner: _____

Superpower *(cont.)*

| First | Silently read "Superpower." You might see words you do not know and read parts you do not understand. Keep reading! Determine what the story is mainly about. |

| Then | Sum up the story. Write the main idea and most important information. If someone reads your summary, that person should know it is this story that you are writing about, not a different story! |

_____

_____

_____

_____

_____

_____

_____

| After That | Read the story again. Use a pencil to circle or mark words you don't know. Note places that confuse you. Underline the main action or idea of each paragraph. |

| Next | Meet with your partner. Help each other find these new words in the text. |

credible   incredible   valuable   invaluable

Read the sentences around the words. Think about how they fit in the whole story. Discuss how the author helped you know what the words meant. Then think about how the prefix *in-* changed the word.

a. The word *credible* means _____

If something is **incredible**, it is unbelievable. I know this, because in the story

_____

_____

b. The word *valuable* means _____

An **invaluable** thing is priceless. It is worth too much to be valued. I know this, because in the story

_____

_____

Your Name: _____

Superpower *(cont.)*

Now Answer the story questions below.

1. Which earbud did Her Majesty adjust? In the box, draw a picture of Her Majesty's face. Circle the ear in which she had the adjusted earbud.

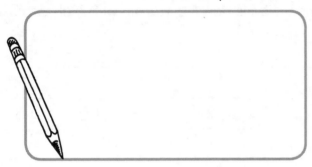

_____

_____

_____

_____

Does everyone have an earbud in this ear? Support your answer with information from the text.

_____

_____

_____

2. Why did Her Majesty check that the boy was not secretly hooked to any device?

_____

_____

3. In paragraph 4, Her Majesty's assistant says, "We may be *sitting on a goldmine* with this child." Look at the underlined phrase. What does he mean when he uses this expression?

_____

_____

How does the story help you know? _____

_____

4. Do you think Her Majesty can read? Defend your answer with evidence from the text.

_____

_____

_____

Your Name: _____

Superpower (cont.)

Then Reread the entire story one last time. Think about what you find out in the last paragraph.

5. *Before* the last paragraph, what hints are you given that people can no longer read?

_____

_____

_____

6. If Her Majesty's assistant had said, "The boy can read," at the very beginning of the story, would the story have been as good? Tell why or why not. You cannot be wrong because it is your opinion, but you must defend your answer.

_____

_____

_____

_____

7. Why might someone say the message of this story is a warning? What is the author warning us about? Explain.

_____

_____

_____

_____

Learn More Research "Voice Command Devices." Write down three facts about the history, use, or development of these devices. In the space below, write what you have learned.

_____

_____

_____

_____

_____

Bridge Standing on End

 John Noble Stearns had a problem. In 1886, Stearns bought a lot that was 21½ feet wide. Stearns then tried to buy one or more adjacent lots, but no one would sell him a lot next to the one he had bought. Unable to purchase adjacent lots, Stearns was told by architects that he could not build the tall building that he wanted to. Stearns' piece of ground was useless.

 Why couldn't Stearns find an architect who could design a building for his lot? His lot was too narrow. It wasn't wide enough. At that time, even the most advanced buildings had exterior walls that had to increase in width toward the bottom. This was so they could support themselves all the way up. If Stearns built the tall building he wanted, he needed walls that were three feet wide at the bottom. He would need space for an elevator and stairs. Once all that space was added up and subtracted from his lot size, Stearns was left with a ground floor that would be less than eight feet wide!

 Stearns ended up going to the architect Bradford Gilbert for help. Gilbert had designed, among other things, railroad bridges and train sheds. This helped Gilbert to think outside the box. After wrestling with the problem for months, Gilbert said that the answer came to him "like a flash." He could support the floors and the outside walls on an iron skeleton. The skeleton would be like an iron bridge standing on end. The exterior walls would be like curtains, resting on the beams of each floor.

 As the building was going up, people stared. They could not believe that a building without thick exterior walls could be so strong. To prove that the building would not fall down, Gilbert climbed its framework in the middle of a huge storm. He then dropped a plumb line. (A plumb line is a line that has a weight at one end.) Despite the huge gusts of wind, the plumb line did not move. This showed that the building was not vibrating or shaking.

5 The Tower Building, as it was so named, was completed in 1889. It was skinny, but it was 11 stories high. It is no longer standing, but today it is considered to be New York City's first skyscraper.

Your Name: _____   Partner: _____

Bridge Standing on End (cont.)

First Silently read "Bridge Standing on End." You might see words you do not know and read parts you do not understand. Keep reading! Determine what the story is mainly about.

Then Sum up the story. Write the main idea and most important information. If someone reads your summary, that person should know it is this story that you are writing about, not a different story!

_____

_____

_____

_____

_____

_____

After That Read the story again. Use a pencil to circle or mark words you don't know. Note places that confuse you. Underline the main action or idea of each paragraph.

Next Meet with your partner. Help each other find these new words in the text.

lot   adjacent   purchase   architect   exterior

Read the sentences around the words. Think about how they fit in the whole story. Think about what the words must mean. Then mark each sentence as **T** (True) or **F** (False). Tell which information in the story helped you know.

_____ **a.** A **lot** is a piece of land. _____

_____

_____ **b.** Our classroom is **adjacent** to the cafeteria. _____

_____

_____ **c.** When you **purchase** something, you build it. _____

_____

_____ **d.** An **architect** is a kind of building. _____

_____

_____ **e.** All walls are **exterior** walls. _____

_____

Your Name: _____

Bridge Standing on End (cont.)

(Now) Answer the story questions below.

1. Was it easy for Gilbert to make the plans for The Tower Building? Explain. Use words from the story to help explain your answer.

_____

_____

_____

_____

2. When and why did Gilbert drop a plumb line?

_____

_____

_____

Why was it important that the plumb line didn't move?

_____

_____

3. In paragraph 3 it says, "This helped Gilbert to think outside the box." What does the expression "to think outside the box" mean in this sentence?

_____

_____

What part of the story helped you know?

_____

_____

_____

4. Did the Tower Building have an elevator? Defend your answer with evidence from the story.

_____

_____

_____

_____

Your Name: _____

Bridge Standing on End (cont.)

Then   Reread the entire story one last time. Tthink about the problem and the solution.

5. What was the problem presented in the story? _____

_____

_____

What was the solution to the problem? _____

_____

_____

6. In which paragraph were you told when The Tower Building was completed? Check a box.

❑ 1   ❑ 2   ❑ 3   ❑ 4   ❑ 5

Why is it important that you are aware of the time period in which this story took place?

_____

_____

Would a building 11 stories high be considered a skyscraper today? Tell why or why not.

_____

_____

_____

7. Look back at the first few sentences of paragraph 1. From this information, what can we infer (guess) about what Stearns was thinking when he purchased the lot. Imagine you are Stearns. Write a few sentences to show your thought process as you are buying the lot.

_____

_____

_____

_____

_____

Learn More   Look in books or online to find out five facts about a skyscraper that it standing today. On the back of this paper, write out your information in paragraph form.

Stranger than Fiction

1 As the students walked into the classroom, each was handed a paper. Ms. Veracity said, "It's a quiz, but it won't be graded. Read and decide which or all are true events. I want you to see that truth can be stranger than fiction." The children bent their heads and began to read studiously.

2 Event One: A gigantic wave raced at a staggering 35 miles per hour. It was 25 feet high and 160 feet wide, and it moved faster than the cars traveling down the street. Unlike ocean waves that only crash in one direction, this wave crashed in every direction. Within seconds, a three-story fire station was flattened, as well as wooden houses, cars, and wagons. The wave wasn't made of water. It was thick brown molasses. Horses and people were trapped in the sticky goo, and it took months to clean the hardening substance from the streets.

3 Event Two: Swedish scientists announced the staggering discovery of a live baby mammoth. Previously, the animal was believed to be extinct for over 10,000 years. A reindeer herder found it still encased in ice on the side of a melting riverbank. Scientists quickly brought the body to the lab. Under close watch, they thawed the ice around the wooly creature. "My heart almost stopped when it moved," one of the scientists reported. "There are cases of frozen frogs not really being dead, but this is a scientific miracle!"

4 Event Three: It did more than rain cats and dogs in England. It rained fish! The fish fell inland, about one-half mile from the sea. These fish were dead, but it has rained live fish as well as frogs at other times and in other places.

5 Ms. Veracity smiled at her students. Events One and Three match my name, she said. They both are true. The Great Molasses Flood took place in Boston in 1919 when a huge tank exploded. Fish and frogs have rained down several times in different places all over the world. Powerful updrafts during thunderstorms can form mini-tornadoes that suck up, carry, and drop fish swimming close to the surface. As for Event Two, while some frogs can survive being frozen for a few months, a mammoth most definitely cannot.

Your Name: _____   Partner: _____

Stranger than Fiction *(cont.)*

First   Silently read "Stranger than Fiction." You might see words you do not know and read parts you do not understand. Keep reading! Determine what the story is mainly about.

Then   Sum up the story. Write the main idea and most important information. If someone reads your summary, that person should know it is this story that you are writing about.

_____

_____

_____

_____

_____

_____

**After
That**   Read the story again. Use a pencil to circle or mark words you don't know. Note places that confuse you. Underline the main action or idea of each paragraph.

Next   Meet with your partner. Help each other find these new words in the text.

veracity   studiously   staggering   extinct   previously

Read the sentences around the words. Think about how they fit in the whole story. Discuss how the author helped you know what the words meant. Then pick one word each. Make sure you each choose a different word. Fill in the blanks.

a.   My partner's word: _____

My partner thinks that in this passage the word must mean _____

_____

I agree because in the passage _____

_____

b.   My word:_____

I think that in this passage this word must mean _____

_____

My partner agrees because in the passage _____

_____

Your Name: _____

Stranger than Fiction (cont.)

Now Answer the story questions below.

1. What did the wave of molasses flatten? Name three things.

_____

_____

_____

_____

2. Why might someone believe Event Two?

_____

_____

_____

3. "It's raining cats and dogs" is an idiom that means "it is raining very hard." Could one ever expect it to truly "rain cats and dogs"? Explain.

_____

_____

How is it possible for it to rain fish? Quote Ms. Veracity as your answer or part of your answer.

_____

_____

_____

4. How long did it take to clean up the molasses?

_____

Why might it be harder to clean up molasses than water? Use evidence from the story in your answer.

_____

_____

_____

_____

Your Name: _____

Stranger than Fiction (cont.)

Then   Reread the entire story one last time. Think about how the paragraphs are organized.

5. How do paragraphs 1 and 5 differ from paragraphs 2, 3, and 4? _____

_____

_____

_____

6. In the first paragaph, did the author tell you how many events would be real? _____

Tell why you think she did or didn't. _____

_____

7. Why do you think the author named the teacher Ms. Veracity? _____

_____

Imagine if the teacher had a name that was an antonym for *veracity*. What might her name be, and how do you think this would have changed the story?

_____

_____

_____

Learn More   Do research to find out five facts about the Great Molasses Flood or strange things that have rained from the sky. Write your facts in paragraph form, making sure you have an introductory and concluding sentence. Use the back of this paper, if needed.

_____

_____

_____

_____

_____

_____

Stuck in Limbo

1   Alfred Mehran was stuck in limbo. His life was in an uncertain state, and for that reason, he could not leave. He was not able to cross the threshold to the outside world. Every day, to get fresh air, Mehran would walk to a door. When it swung open, he would breathe in deeply. He would take deep breaths, but he would never step outside. Mehran did this for 17 years!

2   Mehran was born in Iran, but he wished to settle in the United Kingdom. In 1988, he was on his way, but things went awry. His briefcase containing all of his paperwork, documents, and passport was stolen in Paris, France. Despite the loss of his papers, Mehran boarded a plane for London, England.

3   When the plane landed at London's Heathrow Airport, British authorities refused Mehran entrance. He was sent back to Charles de Gaulle Airport in Paris because he had no passport. Mehran's troubles continued when back in Paris. He was arrested for illegal entry as he had no passport. Usually one is then sent back to their country of origin, but this didn't work for Mehran. Neither Iran nor England would accept him.

4   The case became a legal nightmare. French courts ruled that Mehran had entered the country legally, and so he could not be expelled from the airport. They also said permission to enter France could not be granted. If he left the airport and walked out into the outside world, he would be arrested! Yet Mehran couldn't get on a plane because he could not enter another country without proper papers. Mehran was truly between a rock and a hard place!

5   Polite and courteous, Mehran got up every morning to shave before the airport became crowded with other passengers. He rinsed out his clothes once a week, but only late at night. He made friends with airport employees They enjoyed his presence and brought him food, books, magazines, and newspapers. "He's like a part of the airport. Everyone knows him," one employee said. Mehran read, studied, and wrote in his diary every day of the 17 years he was stranded. Needing to be hospitalized in 2006, Mehran was allowed to leave the airport and live in Paris.

Your Name: _____   Partner: _____

Stuck in Limbo (cont.)

First   Silently read "Stuck in Limbo." You might see words you do not know and read parts you do not understand. Keep reading! Determine what the story is mainly about.

Then   Sum up the story. Write the main idea and most important information. If someone reads your summary, that person should know it is this story that you are writing about.

_____

_____

_____

_____

_____

_____

After That   Read the story again. Use a pencil to circle or mark words you don't know. Note places that confuse you. Underline the main action or idea of each paragraph.

Next   Meet with your partner. Help each other find these new words in the text.

limbo   threshold   awry   expelled   stranded

Read the sentences around the words. Think about how they fit in the whole story. Think about what the words must mean. Then fill in the blanks with the new vocabulary word that fits best. Tell how the story helped you and your partner know.

a. The word _____ means "made to leave." We know this because

_____

b. The word _____ means "crooked." We know this because

_____

c. The word _____ means "an uncertain state." We know this because

_____

d. The word _____ means "stuck." We know this because

_____

e. The word _____ means "edge" or "brink." We know this because

_____

Your Name: _____

Stuck in Limbo (cont.)

Now   Answer the story questions below.

1. What happened to Mehran the first time he flew out of the Paris airport? _____

_____

2. How did the airport employees feel about Mehran? _____

_____

Why do you think they felt this way about him? Use information from the story in your answer.

_____

_____

3. In paragraph 4, it says that that Mehran was "between a rock and a hard place." What is meant by this expression?

_____

Which part of the story helped you know?

_____

_____

4. What did Mehran do while he lived in the airport? Write a diary page as if you were Mehran. Only use information from the story to show what a typical day was like for him.

_____

_____

_____

_____

_____

_____

Your Name: _____

Stuck in Limbo *(cont.)*

Then   Reread the entire story one last time. Think about what paragraph 1 does not tell you.

5. The "5 Ws" refers to the questions that any news article should answer for you. Using information from <u>only paragraph 1</u>, answer these questions. You should only need to use a few words to answer each question.

Who? _____

What? _____

Where? _____

When? _____

Why? _____

6. Answer the big questions again, but this time with information from the entire story. (Some answers may stay the same.)

Who? _____

What? _____

Where? _____

When? _____

Why? _____

7. The mood of a story is the feeling it gives to the reader? What mood do you think the author intended for you to feel as you read the first paragraph? Explain your answer.

_____

_____

After reading the entire story, do you think this was an effective way for the author to begin? Why or why not? In your answer, give your opinion by explaining how this first paragraph did or did not enhance the rest of the story

_____

_____

_____

Learn More   Use books or the Internet to research or find out more information about passports. On the back of this paper, write at least five facts in paragraph form.

Summer Reading

 Sophia was at the end of her rope. She didn't know what to do. She was hired to help take care of her neighbor's two children over the summer. Mrs. Johnson's children were named Jack and Jill, and she wanted Sophia to listen to them read. "They need to practice," Mrs. Johnson said, "but they won't read to me. I'm hoping they won't be as stubborn with you."

 Sophia had tried everything. She had told Jack and Jill how reading was like a magic carpet ride. One could go all over the world, and one could travel to the past and to the future. Jack and Jill reacted to Sophia's words with scorn. "You don't know anything," they sneered.

 Sophia did not sneer back. She did the opposite. With a huge smile on her face, she said sweetly, "If you don't read, I'm going to make the sun disappear." The children stared at Sophia with suspicion. They didn't really believe her, but she looked so certain. There had been no joking tone in her voice. Could she really make the sun disappear? Hadn't Sophia said something about reading and magic?

 Despite their uncertainty, Jack and Jill ran up a hill and began to play in the water of a small spring. Their merriment lasted until the sky began to darken. At first they thought it was only a cloud, but when they looked up, they saw something terrifying. The sun was disappearing! A shadow was spreading across it, leaving nothing but black in its wake. As the sun turned into a big black spot, the sky took on a dark and eerie tinge. Animals sensed that something was wrong and became still. Squirrels hid in their nests, and birds didn't sing a note as they perched uneasily on branches and wires.

 Shaking in fear, Jack and Jill ran down the hill so quickly that they tripped and tumbled. Reaching the bottom, they screamed that they wanted to read. Sophia was more than willing, and she pointed to a sentence in the book she had open and ready. With Sophia helping them sound out new words, the children read. "A total solar eclipse is when the moon passes between the Sun and Earth, causing the moon to completely block out the Sun."

Your Name: _____ Partner: _____

Summer Reading (cont.)

First Silently read "Summer Reading." You might see words you do not know and read parts you do not understand. Keep reading! Determine what the story is mainly about.

Then Sum up the story. Write the main idea and most important information. If someone reads your summary, that person should know it is this story that you are writing about.

_____

_____

_____

_____

_____

_____

After That Read the story again. Use a pencil to circle or mark words you don't know. Note places that confuse you. Underline the main action or idea of each paragraph.

Next Meet with your partner. Help each other find these new words in the text.

      stubborn   reacted   scorn   sneered   suspicion

Read the sentences around the words. Think about how they fit in the whole story. Discuss how the author helped you know what the words meant. Then pick one word each. Make sure you each choose a different word. Fill in the blanks.

a. My partner's word: _____

My partner thinks that in this passage the word must mean _____

_____

I agree because in the passage _____

_____

b. My word: _____

I think that in this passage this word must mean _____

_____

My partner agrees because in the passage _____

_____

Your Name: _____

Summer Reading *(cont.)*

Now   Answer the story questions below.

1. Why did Mrs. Johnson feel she needed to hire Sophia? _____

_____

2. In paragraph 4, what did the animals sense? _____

_____

How did squirrels and birds act? Quote words from the story for your answer for each.

_____

_____

_____

_____

_____

_____

3. The story starts by saying Sophia is "at the end of her rope." What does this expression mean as it is used in the story?

_____

_____

Which parts of the story helped you know? _____

_____

_____

4. Do you think Sophia knew there was going to be a solar eclipse that day? Explain why you think so. Give at least two reasons.

_____

_____

_____

_____

Your Name: _____

Summer Reading *(cont.)*

Then   Reread the entire story one last time. As you read, think about how the last paragraph relates to the rest of the passage.

5. If you stopped reading after paragraph 4, why might you think this is a story that belongs in a book of scary tales?

_____

_____

6. Do you think Jack and Jill are now going to be more willing to practice their reading? Tell why or why not. You cannot be wrong because it is your opinion, but you must defend your answer with information from the story.

_____

_____

_____

7. Choose one of the following to answer:

◆   Did this story remind you of any other story (or stories) you have read? If so, explain. Name the story or stories it reminded you of. Tell which parts of this story seemed familiar to you.

◆   In this story, Sophia says that reading is like a magic carpet ride that can take you all over the world or into the past or future. Name a book you have read that takes place in a different part of the world or in the past or future. Explain how that book took you to a different place or time.

_____

_____

_____

_____

_____

_____

Learn More   Look in books or online to find out three more facts about eclipses. On the back of this paper, write your findings.

The Fifth Time

 There is a saying that goes, "the third time is the charm." It wasn't true for Diana Nyad. Nyad's third attempt was a failure. So was her fourth. Most people would have stopped trying, but Nyad wouldn't. Despite the fact that she had almost died and suffered horrible and intense pain, Nyad continued to try to do something that no one had ever done before. It took her 35 years, but she finally succeeded on her fifth attempt.

 Nyad successfully swam from Havana, Cuba, to Key West, Florida, without a protective shark cage around her. It took Nyad almost 53 hours of nonstop swimming to cover the 103 miles across the strait. Previous attempts had failed in large part because of excruciatingly painful jellyfish stings. One sting on her tongue almost caused her to suffocate. On her final and ultimate attempt, Nyad wore a special mask that covered her entire face, a full-body suit, gloves, and booties to protect her from jellyfish stings. People also tried to collect all the jellyfish in front of her and move them away as she swam.

 Nyad says her success was a team effort. She did not swim in a protective cage, but she had help. "Shark divers" took turns swimming around her. These swimmers carried special "zappers" to ward off predators. Aides, using a long pole, provided her with food and high-energy drinks. People also helped her determine when the ocean would be at its warmest temperature, and when there would be the least likelihood of storms.

 At one point while swimming, Nyad hallucinated. She saw the yellow brick road from *The Wizard of Oz.* She said it was right below her, under the water. She said she saw the Seven Dwarfs (from the story *Snow White and the Seven Dwarfs*) marching on the road. She said the dwarfs were very helpful, as she was able to follow them for well over three hours.

 The nights were treacherous. Nyad said that it was "Absolutely inky black out there." At one point after the wind picked up, Nyad said, "I started taking in large walls of seawater. I started vomiting into the mask and kicking hard to keep my face above water."

Your Name: _____ Partner: _____

The Fifth Time *(cont.)*

First — Silently read "The Fifth Time." You might see words you do not know and read parts you do not understand. Keep reading! Determine what the story is mainly about.

Then — Sum up the story. Write the main idea and most important information. If someone reads your summary, that person should know it is this story that you are writing about.

_____

_____

_____

_____

_____

_____

After That — Read the story again. Use a pencil to circle or mark words you don't know. Note places that confuse you. Underline the main action or idea of each paragraph.

Next — Meet with your partner. Help each other find these new words in the text.

| strait | excruciatingly | ultimate | hallucinated | treacherous |

Read the sentences around the words. Think about how they fit in the whole story. Think about what the words mean and decide how the story helps you know the following things:

a. A **strait** is a narrow passage of water connecting two seas or oceans.

_____

_____

b. An **excruciating** pain is one that is intense and really hurts. _____

_____

c. The **ultimate** time you do something is the last time you do it. _____

_____

d. If you **hallucinate**, you are seeing things that aren't really there. _____

_____

e. When something is **treacherous**, it is very dangerous. _____

_____

Your Name: _____

The Fifth Time (cont.)

Now   Answer the story questions below.

1. How did Nyad protect herself from sharks? _____

_____

The story mentions another way she could have protected herself but chose not to. Name it?

_____

2. Describe what Nyad saw when she was hallucinating? _____

_____

_____

Was this a helpful hallucination? Tell why or why not, using evidence from the text.

_____

_____

3. The saying "the third time is the charm" is part of the first sentence. What does this saying mean in the way it is used here?

_____

How does the story help you know? _____

_____

4. The story mentions jellyfish. What problems did they cause for Nyad? What did she do to try to combat these problems? For each, name two. Complete the diagram.

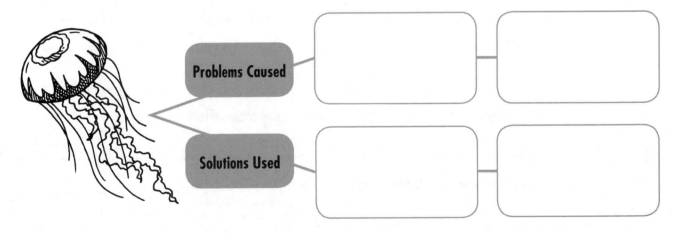

Problems Caused

Solutions Used

Your Name: _____

The Fifth Time *(cont.)*

Then   Reread the entire story one last time. Think about how the title relates to the passage.

5. After reading <u>only the first paragraph</u> of the story, what do you know about Nyad's fifth attempt?

_____

_____

When exactly do you find out what she was trying to do that took her five times to accomplish? (Name the line and the paragraph in which you learn this information.)

_____

6. You want to read an adventure story or one about swimming. You look through a book's Table of Contents for a story that might interest you. Why might you skip this story with its current title of "The Fifth Time"?

_____

_____

Write another title for this story. Create one that would catch the eye of someone who is looking for story about adventure or swimming.

_____

Explain why your title would grab a reader's attention.

_____

_____

7. Think about the people who helped Nyad along on her journey. Write a short diary entry from one of these people's perspectives. Pretend you are that person. Write what you did that day to help Nyad accomplish her goal. Include information from the story.

_____

_____

_____

_____

 Learn More   Nyad wore protective clothing because of the box jellyfish. Find out about this creature and its painful sting. On the back of this paper, write your findings in paragraph form.

The Smile Cure

 "#1: The more you take, the more you leave behind. #2: Give it food, and it will live; give it water, and it will die. #3: It is lighter than a feather, yet the strongest man can't hold it for much more than a minute. #4: What can you catch but can't throw? #5: As I walked along the path, I saw something with four fingers and one thumb, but it was not flesh, fish, bone, or bird."

The students in Mr. Nakamura's class stared at their teacher in stunned silence. His strange behavior was so shocking that they were speechless. He usually started the day's lesson with a review of math facts. He didn't spout nonsense! The only reason the students weren't completely terrified was because of the expression on his face. He was grinning from ear to ear.

 Mr. Nakamura soon explained. "We smile when we are happy, but there's more to a smile than showing happiness. Smiling can help cure unhappiness, because it makes us feel happier! If we force a smile, we will be happier and want to smile! Through studies, scientists have found that when we smile, our brains respond in a certain way. Smiling — even if it's forced — makes us feel better. It can even make us feel less pain! Tests showed that people who were smiling felt less pain. People who were frowning felt more pain!"

"Now that scientists have proved the worth of smiling," Mr. Nakamura said, "I've come to the conclusion that we must smile more. We will force ourselves to smile even when we are doing something that is new and novel. We will smile even when things are difficult and challenging. I decided that to kick off our first day of smiling more, I would entertain you with some riddles. So even if you don't know the answers to my riddles, smile!"

 The students couldn't help but smile in relief, because they were no longer worried that their teacher had lost his mind. What they thought was nonsense were riddles! After talking among themselves, they told Mr. Nakamura that the answers to the riddles were footsteps, fire, your breath, a cold, and a glove. When told that their answers were correct, the children smiled. "No need to force smiles over this assignment," they said.

Your Name: _____   Partner: _____

The Smile Cure *(cont.)*

First   Silently read "The Smile Cure." You might see words you do not know and read parts you do not understand. Keep reading! Determine what the story is mainly about.

Then   Sum up the story. Write the main idea and most important information. If someone reads your summary, that person should know it is this story that you are writing about, not a different story!

_____

_____

_____

_____

_____

_____

After That   Read the story again. Use a pencil to circle or mark words you don't know. Note places that confuse you. Underline the main action or idea of each paragraph.

Next   Meet with your partner. Help each other find these new words in the text.

stunned   spout   cure   novel   relief

Read the sentences around the words. Think about how they fit in the whole story. Then match the words to their synonyms. Tell which part of the story help you and your partner know you are right.

a. The word _____ means "new." We know this because

_____

b. The word _____ means "gush." We know this because

_____

c. The word _____ means "astonished." We know this because

_____

d. The word _____ means "treatment." We know this because

_____

e. The word _____ means "comfort." We know this because

_____

Your Name: _____

The Smile Cure *(cont.)*

 Answer the story questions below.

1. How does Mr. Nakamura's class usually start? Use a complete sentence.

_____

_____

2. Look at the pictures. For each, rewrite the riddle that Mr. Nakamura uses to describe them?

 _____

_____

_____

_____

 _____

_____

_____

3. Near the end of paragraph 4, Mr. Nakamura says that he has decided "to kick off" the day. What is meant by this expression the way it is used here?

_____

Which parts of the story helped you know?

_____

_____

4. Why might it help to smile if you get a shot? Use evidence from the story in your answer.

_____

_____

_____

Your Name: _____

The Smile Cure *(cont.)*

Then Reread the entire story one last time. As you read, think about how the first paragraph relates to the rest of the passage.

5. In the second paragraph, you are told that the students think that Mr. Nakamura is spouting nonsense. Did you think the first paragraph was nonsense the first time you read it? Were you confused like the students? Tell why or why not. Use a line or two from the paragraph to prove your point.

_____

_____

_____

_____

_____

6. How did your understanding of paragraph 1 change by the end of the story?

_____

_____

_____

What was your favorite riddle? Why?

_____

_____

_____

7. What might Mr. Nakamura say to you if you are unhappy with these questions? Defend your answer with information from the story.

_____

_____

_____

Learn More Think up or find five riddles. Write them on the back of this paper, and then try to stump the class with them. Remember to smile as you do this task and also when you try to solve your schoolmates' riddles!

Working the Tempest

1 The glass had to remain clear. If salt, snow, or ice accumulated on it, the light still had to be seen. The light had to remain steady and strong, otherwise people could die. George Easterbrook was a second assistant keeper at a lighthouse, and he was determined to keep the glass clear and people safe.

2 George worked at Cape Disappointment Lighthouse in Washington. The lighthouse was a 53-foot-tall brick tower. During a powerful tempest in 1869, the 17-year-old Easterbrook went out at midnight to clear the glass. A gust of wind blew the door shut, locking George out. He was stuck on the narrow balcony, the wind and cold from the fierce storm raging around him.

3 George cleaned the panes, but all the while worried thoughts raced through his head. He couldn't wait to be saved by the keeper who would arrive in the morning, because in the next two hours the light would go out. If a ship hit the rocks, George would be the one responsible for the loss of lives.

4 Knowing he had to get down, George grabbed hold of a one-inch-thick copper wire and began his dangerous descent. The wire was part of a lightning rod, and it was only fixed to the top of the tower. Over and over, strong gusts of wind caused George to swing back and forth like a pendulum on a clock. As he twirled and twisted in mid-air, he never knew if he would lose his grip or if the slender copper thread he was holding onto would snap in two.

5 When George's feet finally touched earth, he couldn't let go of the wire. The ground was too steep. He would tumble down the rocks into the water. He had to wait for a huge blast of wind to swing him to a safer part of the tower, and then he had to let go at just the right moment. It took the last of his strength, but he managed. Once on the ground, he was so spent that he blacked out. When he woke up, he raced up the stairs to the lantern room. The light was dim, but it wasn't out. It had been a close call, but George had done his job. A few weeks later, he resigned. Instead of becoming a head lighthouse keeper or even a first-assistant, he became a medical doctor.

Your Name: _____

Working the Tempest *(cont.)*

For this activity, work in groups of four. If your group has fewer than four members, share the Mr./Ms. Future task. Begin by deciding who will perform each task.

Title	Student's Name	What Is Your Task?
Mr./Ms. Meaning		Explain the meanings of unfamiliar words.
Mr./Ms. Plot		Summarize what is happening in the passage.
Mr./Ms. Ask		Ask important questions about the passage.
Mr./Ms. Future		Guess what will happen next in the passage.

First) Read paragraphs 1–2 of "Working the Tempest." Then stop reading and do the following:

Mr./Ms. Meaning: Define these words for your group: *accumulated, tempest, gust,* and *balcony.*

Mr./Ms .Plot: Summarize paragraphs 1 and 2. Tell how knowing what *accumulated, tempest, gust,* and *balcony* mean helps you know what is going on.

Mr./Ms .Ask: Check your group's understanding by asking them a question about the glass and George.

Mr./Ms. Future: Guess what will happen to George next. Will the light remain steady and strong?

Next) Read paragraphs 1–4 of "Working the Tempest." Then stop reading and do the following:

Mr./Ms. Meaning: Define these words for your group: *wire, descent,* and *pendulum.*

Mr./Ms. Plot: Remind the group what happened in paragraphs 1 and 2. Then sum up paragraphs 3 and 4.

Mr./Ms. Ask: Ask a what/where/why/how question (one each) about George and his situation.

Mr./Ms. Future: Think about George holding on for dear life. Will someone come to help him? Will he fall into the water? Will he keep the light going?

Then) Read the entire passage from start to finish. As a group, do the following:

♦ Discuss the ending of the story. Are you surprised by what happened? What did you think would happen? How do you think the real story might have ended differently?

♦ Find and share some quotes that help you understand the danger George was in.

♦ Talk about the author's purpose in writing this story. What do you think the author wanted you to learn about or think about?

♦ Are lighthouses as important as they once were? Why or why not?

Finally) On a separate piece of paper, write a short summary of your group's discussion.

Octavia's Report

 Octavia's report was on human blood. She didn't choose this topic. It was assigned. At first Octavia was unhappy with her topic, but as she delved more into the subject matter, she became fascinated.

 "If a human being weighed 100 pounds, seven pounds of his or her weight would be from blood. Human blood contains red blood cells, white blood cells, and platelets. The red and white blood cells and platelets float in a yellow liquid. The yellow liquid is called blood plasma. Blood plasma is 90% water. The other 10% is various nutrients, electrolytes, gases, proteins, glucose, and hormones.

 "Blood travels through blood vessels. Arteries, capillaries, and veins are all blood vessels. If you laid a human's blood vessels end-to-end, they would measure about 100,000 km, or 60,000 miles! If you're not dumbfounded, you should be! Why should you be astonished? You should be amazed, because that distance is approximately 2.5 times Earth's circumference. In other words, an adult human has enough blood vessels to circle Earth two and a half times!

 "Red blood cells have the important job of carrying oxygen around the body. It takes a red blood cell about 30 seconds to make a complete circuit. In a human, red blood cells develop in the bone marrow. Then they circulate for about 120 days. Red blood cells are what make human blood look red. That's because they contain a protein. The protein is called hemoglobin. Hemoglobin contains iron. The hemoglobin combines with oxygen, and when this happens, it makes the blood look red."

 Octavia raised two of her arms. She said, "It is strange to think of blood being red. I would be terrified if I cut myself, and I saw red. Blood should be blue, like ours! The blue color is because our blood is copper-based rather than iron-based. Copper-based blood is much more efficient at transporting oxygen. That's very important when it comes to surviving in the deep ocean. With my eight arms over my three hearts, I salute my blue blood!"

Your Name: _____

Octavia's Report (cont.)

For this activity, work in groups of four. If your group has fewer than four members, share the Mr./Ms. Future task. Begin by deciding who will perform each task.

Title	Student's Name	What Is Your Task?
Mr./Ms. Meaning		Explain the meaning of unfamiliar words.
Mr./Ms. Plot		Summarize what is happening in the passage.
Mr./Ms. Ask		Ask important questions about the passage.
Mr./Ms. Future		Guess what will happen next in the passage.

First Read paragraphs 1 and 2 of "Octavia's Report." Then stop reading and do the following:

Mr./Ms. Meaning: Define these words for your group: *assigned*, *delved*, and *plasma*.

Mr./Ms. Plot: Summarize what happened in paragraphs 1 and 2. Tell how knowing what *assigned*, *delved*, and *plasma* mean helps you know what is going on.

Mr./Ms. Ask: Check your group's understanding by asking a question about Octavia's report and a blood fact.

Mr./Ms. Future: Guess what is going to happen next. Is Octavia only going to talk about blood? What other things might she say about it?

Next Read paragraphs 1–4 of "Octavia's Report." Then stop reading and do the following:

Mr./Ms. Meaning: Define these words for your group: *dumbfounded*, *circumference*, and *circuit*.

Mr./Ms. Plot: Review paragraphs 1 and 2. Then sum up paragraphs 3 and 4.

Mr./Ms. Ask: Ask a who/what/where/why/how question (one each) about the report.

Mr./Ms. Future: Think about how Octavia will conclude her report. Will she sum up the information? Will she ask you to donate blood? Will she tell you that it would take one bite each of 1,200,000 mosquitoes to drain a human of blood?

Then Read the entire passage from start to finish. As a group, do the following:

- Discuss the ending of the story. Did it surprise you? Did you learn anything?

- Find and share some quotes from the passage that help you understand what kinds of blood vessels there are in human bodies and how long they stretch.

- Talk about the author's purpose in writing this story. What do you think the author wanted you to learn about or think about?

- Think like a scientist: Why might an octopus need three hearts instead of just one?

Finally On a separate piece of paper, write a short summary of your group's discussion.

"Flashlights Skyward" (pages 8–11)

Summary: The Leadville 100 is a grueling endurance race. Tarahumara runners from Mexico came to race three times. The first time they lost because they didn't even know what a flashlight was. They easily won the second and third times.

Vocabulary: a. False; b. True; c. False; d. False; e. True

1. They dropped out before the halfway point. They suffered from culture shock.
2. The race is 100 miles, so it's 50 miles in and 50 miles out.
3. It takes place deep in the middle of the mountains. It has high mountains, rugged trails, ice and snow, etc.
4. 1st picture: brand-name running shoes; 2nd picture: sandals; They "tore the shoes off their feet and threw them away" at the first check-in station.
5. Information is given about the Leadville Trail 100 Run; information is given about the Tarahumara racing in the Leadville Trail 100 Run.
6. She wanted you to understand what a hard race it was and to picture the Tarahumara failing but then winning so easily.

"Mystery Solved" (pages 12–15)

Summary: Ada and Ethan want to be detectives, and their father advises that they read a lot. They solve two mysteries because of what they learned while reading.

Vocabulary: b. Summer firmly, or insists that the bill is hers; c. The docent is a volunteer guide, and volunteers aren't paid; d. Ada claims the picture is fake; e. Ada says that a food's origins are where it came from.

1. The painting was said to be from 14th century France. Potatoes and tomatoes were not brought to Europe until the late 15th century.
2. even; "I know because all books have odd-numbered pages on the right."
4. The docent says that the painting depicts a typical scene from a 14th-century country kitchen in France, and the woman is kneading bread.
5. Reading is very important, because it provides a foundation for any kind of work; the characters use information learned from books to solve two mysteries.

"New Flag Needed!" (pages 16–19)

Summary: National flags identify countries. Almost all countries have rectangular flags. The flags of some countries are very similar to the flags of others.

Vocabulary: horizontal = "going across, from side to side"; displayed = "shown"; retain = "keep"; tricolor = "made of three colors"

1. They discovered that Haiti had the same flag, and they needed to make theirs different. The crown was added onto the blue; the story tells us that the crown was added in the top left corner, and the top half of the flag is blue.
2. Per the information given in the story, students should draw a ship with a rectangular flag (not square) featuring a cross in the center.
3. It means that something really looks identical or alike; if you just looked quickly at the flags from Monaco and Indonesia, you would think they were the same.
4. from left to right: Republic of Ireland = green, white, orange; Ivory Coast = orange, white, green.

"Garrulous Gabby" (pages 20–23)

Summary: A girl hates her nickname — Garrulous Gabby — which she has been given because she talks so much. She wins a story contest when she writes about a lonely girl who learns to listen. She is so surprised, she is speechless.

Vocabulary: a. False; b. True; c. False; d. True

1. Gabby; she feels it had a wonderful and happy ring to it.
2. At first, the advice seems to have fallen on deaf ears because Gabriela keeps talking. The story Gabriela writes seems to show that she finally understands her mom's advice.

3. It means that she got really hot and angry; she says it when she is complaining angrily about how she despises being called "garrulous."
4. An elephant's ears are big and thin with lots of veins. When an elephant flaps them, this action can cool a lot of blood.
5. a. It's an adjective, because it describes something (a person); b. no; c. The author shows you its meaning by having the character of Gabriela talk so much while saying so little.
6. The big lesson is that conversations can't be one-sided. As Gabriela's mother says, "You need to learn to listen."

"Knocked Flat" (pages 24–27)

Summary: One is asked if children should be shielded before being introduced to an author's cautionary poems. Details are given about the author and his poems.

Vocabulary: deeds = "things one does"; dire = "terrible or horrible"; consequences = "results"; abhors = "hates"; prolific = "productive, creative"

1. She is knocked flat and killed when a marble statue falls on her that was above the door she slammed.
2. Yes, because one of his cautionary tales is about "Sarah Byng, who could not read and was tossed into a thorny hedge by a bull."
3. It means that everything is rosy and good, and nothing bad is happening.
4. *Quote:* "because my children are howling for pearls and caviar"; *Meaning:* I need money to raise my children, and they ask for a lot of expensive things; *Examples:* Pearls and caviars are luxury items that are very expensive.
6. No, because she says "the jury is still out." It is still being decided.

"Hard to Believe" (pages 28–31)

Summary: Parents want grown-up time, but they keep hearing wild laughing from their children's room. The children keep claiming it is a hyena under the bed. The parents get angry and don't believe the children, and then they meet a talking crocodile.

Vocabulary: a. innocent; b. ridiculous; d. wearily; e. irate

1. They heard wild laughter, and they wanted the children to go to sleep.
2. They thought the children were lying. They thought it was a ridiculous story.
3. It means they came in angrily, quickly, and with unstoppable force; the parents say they are getting madder, and they want the laughter to stop.
4. Students should draw a crocodile on a couch and use words like *surprised.* Mrs. Martinez stopped suddenly, made funny sounds, and had a shaky hand.
5. Accept appropriate responses. Before paragraph 5, there was no reason to think the children were telling the truth.

"Movie-Watching Locusts" (pages 32–35)

Summary: A scientist studied locusts' brains while they watched *Star Wars* to learn why they don't crash into each other. Her goal is to make cars that avoid accidents.

Vocabulary: solitary = "only one, alone"; swarm = "a large group moving together"; consume = "eat"; collision = "crash"; obstacle = "something in your way"

1. Rind wants to design a collision-avoidance system for cars; she wants to make cars that won't crash into each other.
2. Locusts are small animals, and a roar is a really loud noise. For small wings to make a roaring sound, there has got to be a whole lot of them!
3. *Star Wars;* It has lots of spaceships coming at the viewer from all directions. This helped show how locusts' special neurons reacted to the movement of the ships.
4. No, because it is still only successful nine out of ten times. There would still be too many accidents.
5. Paragraph 1 is mainly about how destructive the locust can be when it swarms. Huge swarms can leave nothing but bare ground.

"Mind Reading" (pages 36–39)

Summary: Josie tells Cesar she can read his mind and asks him do some calculations. After correctly guessing what Cesar is thinking, she explains how the trick works.

1. If Josie's instructions were followed correctly, everyone will get the number 4, and D is the corresponding letter in the alphabet.

2. Step 2: $9 \times 5 = 45$; Step 3: $4 + 5 = 9$; Step 4: $9 - 5 = 4$

3. It was really easy; Cesar spoke confidently when asked to add the digits in his answer and subtract five. If it were hard, he wouldn't be sure he was right.

4. Students might say kangaroo. Denmark ends with a *k*, and kangaroo is probably the most well-known animal that begins with that letter.

5. 1. Pick a number from 1–10; 2. Multiply by 9; 3. Add digits; 4. Subtract 5, match to corresponding letter in the alphabet; 5. Think of a country that starts with letter; 6. Think of animal that starts with the second letter of country.

"Principal's Office" (pages 40–43)

Summary: The author's favorite story about being sent to the principal's office is from an autobiographical book. The story goes that a boy's pet owl escapes its cage, flies into his classroom, and badly scares his teacher.

Vocabulary: a. *avian* = "bird"; b. *furious* = "mad"; c. *twine* = "string"; d. *deter* = "discourage"; e. *scattered* = "strewn"

1. Farley Mowat; Mowat writes about his own life and his pet owls.

2. He got to the schoolyard as the two-minute bell was ringing, and he tied Wol to his handlebars before he ran in.

3. It means that Mowat pedaled really fast; He continued to race to school, and was going so fast he had to skid to a stop.

4. *wild:* owls aren't domesticated, Wol ripped open its cage; *tame:* it landed on Mowat's shoulder, it didn't bite or claw him, it let Mowat tie him with twine.

5. From the title, one migh expect that the story will be about what happens inside a principal's office. After paragraph 1, one might expect to learn more about what the person did to get in trouble (and how owls are involved).

6. The author describes the huge rush of air as the owl lands, the way the bike skids into the schoolyard, the sound the owl makes on the window, the way the papers on the teacher's desk scatter as the owl slides across it, etc.

"Updated Fairy Tale" (pages 44–47)

Summary: A set of twins have jealous siblings who strand them in the middle of a forest. The twins end up on a movie set, and they get to be part of the movie.

Vocabulary: b. True; c. False; d. False; e. True

1. fraternal; identical; Identical twins look the same, but fraternal twins do not.

2. It makes it easier for everyone, because those who are lost don't wander in circles, and rescuers don't have to look in places they have already searched.

3. They are very tired and have "paid" out all they can in energy and effort; in the next sentences, we are told they are tired, dirty, hungry, and about to collapse.

4. Answers will vary. Yes, because didn't tell on siblings and waited for movie to be on television; No, because didn't hug a tree and wait for rescuers.

5. *Beginning:* Once upon a time; *Ending:* happily ever after; Someone not familiar with fairy tales would not be familiar with these phrases.

"Lung Capacity How-To" (pages 48–51)

Summary: Lungs are organs that take in oxygen and release carbon dioxide. Exercising can increase lung capacity. We can use simple materials to determine capacity.

Vocabulary: *depths* = "down where it is deep"; *primary* = "main, most important"; *function* = "purpose"; *current* = "present, right now"; *capacity* = "size, ability"

1. Their lungs have enough capacity or can take in enough air.

2. Your lungs transport oxygen from the air we breathe into our bloodstream while taking away carbon dioxide.

3. It is a group of tissues that performs a specific purpose or group of functions.

4. SCUBA divers wear equipment, while free divers do not; free diving requires more, because the only oxygen one gets is the breath taken before diving.

5. It is showing you how to test your lung capacity; paragraphs 3 and 4.

6. *Suggestions:* Title = How-To Test Lung Capacity; Materials = large bowl, large plastic bottle with lid or cap, bendy straw; Step 1 = Fill the bowl about half full with water; Step 2 = Fill the bottle with water and put on the lid; Step 3 = Turn the bottle upside down and put it in the bowl; Step 4 = Remove the lid, keeping the spout in the water; Step 5 = Put the bendy straw in the spout and blow.

7. They are mostly about lung capacity, what it is, and how you can improve it.

"Stay Clear!" (pages 52–55)

Summary: Two partners are feeling scared amidst poisonous and dangerous plants. It turns out that they are in the botanical gardens and are protected by glass walls.

Vocabulary: *shuddered* = "trembled, shook"; *tremble* = "shaking"; *botanists* = "people who study plants"; *potent* = "strong and powerful"; *foul* = "disgusting"

1. It is covered in hollow poisonous hairs that penetrate the skin on contact. The poison can feel like burning acid, and the pain can last for two years.

2. Iits thorns are like a shark's teeth; Henry says, "You'd be slashed to pieces."

3. They are going from a bad situation to one that may be even worse; as they leave the dangerous blackberries, they smell something that may be worse.

4. *Possible answers: No* = Maya says, "We'd have to be separated from some plants by glass walls and hold our noses around others." This makes it sound like they are two different things, and it would be hard to smell through a glass wall. Maya says that parts of it can be eaten, so they can touch it without danger; *Yes* = They are in the part of the gardens where there are dangerous plants, and botanists wouldn't want anyone to eat anything poisonous.

5. You might think Maya and Henry were in real danger, especially as Henry says, "out of the frying pan and into the fire."

"Worth Billions" (pages 56–59)

Summary: The writer thinks colonizing Mars is worth the high cost and gives several reasons, from the invention of helpful things to the survival of the human species.

Vocabulary: *colonize* = "send people to a new place to make a home"; *astronomical* = "really big"; *shortsighted* = "not thinking to the future"; *detect* = "find, discover"

1. It is bigger; two-thirds of Earth's surface is covered by water.

2. Three: survival of species; finding life on Mars; improving life on Earth

3. It is very expensive; you are told that the price is astronomical and will cost hundreds of billions of dollars.

4. Students can choose three of the following to illustrate and consider: microchips, scratch-resistant glasses, water filters, joysticks, cordless tools, smoke detectors.

5. It is mainly about giving interesting facts about Mars and comparing it to Earth. It serves as an introduction for the rest of the passage.

6. "Should we colonize Mars?"; the answer is an opinion; the author uses facts to defend her opinion, but it is still what she thinks.

"Superpower" (pages 60–63)

Summary: Her Majesty doesn't believe a boy has a superpower. In this society where everyone communicates by listening, a boy who can read is said to have powers.

Vocabulary: *credible* = "believable"; *valuable* = "of great worth"

1. Students should draw a person and circle her right ear; not everyone has one in this ear, only government officials are allowed right earbuds.

2. She wanted to be sure he wasn't simply repeating what he was hearing.

3. He means that the child may be very valuable and of great worth; he says the child's power is so valuable, he is invaluable.

4. No, she can't. She listened to the report about the boy five times and watched it, and she thought that reading was a superpower.

5. Her Majesty listens to the report and watches the performance; everyone has earbuds attached, because it is the only way they communicate.

"Bridge Standing on End" (pages 64–67)

Summary: A man bought a narrow lot and needed an architect to figure out a new way to support a narrow building. New York's first skyscraper was built on this lot.

Vocabulary: a. T, b. T or F, depending on school; c. F; d. F; e. F

1. It was not easy; although the idea came to him "like a flash," he "wrestled with the problem for months" beforehand.

2. He dropped it in the middle of a huge storm so he could prove the building wouldn't fall down; it showed that the building wasn't moving, even though there were huge gusts of winds.

3. It means he thought in a new, nontraditional way; instead of thick walls, he used an internal skeleton like a bridge standing on its end to support the building.

4. Yes, you are told in the paragraph 1 that Stearns would be left with less than eight feet of space after the wall, elevator, and stair footage was subtracted.

5. *Problem:* Stearns only had a narrow lot, which would have left him with less than eight feet of floor space; *Solution:* The architect designed a steel framework on which the exterior walls rested like curtains on the beams.

6. paragraph 5; it isn't a modern problem at all, so the story wouldn't make sense and you wouldn't understand how important and new Gilbert's idea was.

"Stranger than Fiction" (pages 68–71)

Summary: A teacher has her students decide which of three events is true. The story tells us more about the true events and explains why the other one is false.

Vocabulary: *veracity* = "truth"; *studiously* = "thoughtfully, quietly studying"; *staggering* = "amazing, deeply shocking"; *extinct* = "dead, all gone"; *previously* = "happening before"

1. It flattened a three-story fire station, wooden houses, cars, and wagons.

2. There are some kinds of frogs that can survive being frozen for several months, as well as reindeer herders finding bodies of mammoths in melting ice.

3. No, because lots of cats and dogs would not likely be picked up in the way that fish "swimming close to the surface" would be.

4. It took months. Molasses is sticky, and then as it dries, it gets hard. Also, it doesn't evaporate the way water does.

5. Paragraph 1 acts as the introduction and 5 as the conclusion. The other paragraphs are the body, each focusing on one event.

6. No. She said, "which or all are true events."

"Stuck in Limbo" (pages 72–75)

Summary: A man from Iran became stranded in a Paris airport for 17 years. His documents were stolen, and if he left, he would be arrested. He was always clean and courteous. He was allowed to go free in 2006 when he needed to be hospitalized.

Vocabulary: a. expelled; b. awry; c. limbo; d. stranded; e. threshold

1. He landed in London but was sent back to Paris because he didn't have papers.

2. They liked him. One employee said, "He's like a part of the airport. Everyone knows him"; the story tells us that he was "polite and courteous."

3. It means that you're facing two very difficult and unpleasant choices; before this expression, the story shows that every option Mehran has will lead to his arrest.

4. Diary entries might include: shaving, washing clothes, reading, studying, writing, taking breaths when doors open, receiving things from airport workers.

5. *Who:* Alfred Mehran; *What:* stuck in limbo; *Where:* inside; *When:* date unsure, but 17 years; *Why:* could not leave

6. *Who:* Alfred Mehran; *What:* stuck in French airport due to legal nightmare; *Where:* Charles de Gaulle Airport, Paris; *When:* 1988 to 2006; *Why:* lost papers

"Summer Reading" (pages 76–79)

Summary: A babysitter tells two kids she will make the Sun disappear if they don't read. There is a total solar eclipse, and the kids think she did it, so they want to read.

Vocabulary: *stubborn* = "not willing to do something"; *reacted* = "responded to something"; *scorn* = "making fun of something"; *sneered* = "to made a nasty face at, made fun of"; *suspicion* = "not sure of, having doubt"

1. Jack and Jill needed to practice reading. They wouldn't read to her, and she was hoping they would read to Sophia.

2. They sensed that something was wrong; squirrels: hid in their nests; birds: didn't sing a note as they perched uneasily on branches and wires.

3. It means that she has lost her patience. She doesn't know what to do anymore; no matter what she says, she can't get Jack and Jill to read.

4. She probably wouldn't say she could make the Sun disappear if she didn't know there was going to be an eclipse; also, she had the page ready for them to read.

5. Sophia makes a threat, and it seems as if it is coming true; the author uses words like *terrifying, dark,* and *eerie.*

"The Fifth Time" (pages 80–83)

Summary: Diana Nyad made five attempts to swim from Cuba to Florida. Even though her last attempt was challenging, it was successful because of her team of helpers.

1. She had a team of "shark divers" who had special "zappers" that swam with her; she chose not to swim in a protective shark cage.

2. She saw the Seven Dwarfs marching down the yellow brick road; it was helpful, because Nyad was able to follow the dwarves for over three hours.

3. It means that the third time you do something, it works out; in the story, it says that this time it wasn't true, because she failed on her third attempt.

4. *Problems:* excruciating pain, sting on tongue almost caused suffocation; *Solutions:* wore full head mask and body suit, had people clear the area

5. You only know that she succeeded at something on her fifth attempt. It is not until the first line of the second paragraph that we learn what she accomplished.

6. "The Fifth Time" could refer to anything that was done five times; it does not tell you in any way that it is about swimming or adventure.

"The Smile Cure" (pages 84–87)

Summary: A teacher asks his students lots of riddles instead of reviewing math facts. He says that smiling makes one feel better. His riddles make everyone smile more.

Vocabulary: a. novel; b. spout; c. stunned; d. cure; e. relief

1. He usually starts class with a review of math facts.

2. *footsteps:* "The more you take, the more you leave behind."; *fire:* "Give it food and it will live; give it water and it will die."

3. "to start something"; he is using riddles to start off the week of smiling more.

4. You would feel less pain. Evens a forced smile would help one will feel less pain.

The lessons and activities included in *Close Reading with Text-Dependent Questions* meet the following Common Core State Standards for grade 5. (©Copyright 2010. National Governors Association Center for Best Practices and Council of Chief State School Officers. All rights reserved.)

The code for each standard covered in this resource is listed in the table below and on page 96. The codes are listed in boldface, and the unit numbers of the activities that meet that standard are listed in regular type. For more information about the Common Core State Standards and for a full listing of the descriptions associated with each code, go to *http://www.corestandards.org/* or visit *http://www.teachercreated.com/standards/*.

Here is an example of an English Language Arts (ELA) code and how to read it:

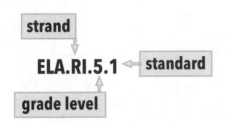

ELA Strands	
L	= Language
W	= Writing
RI	= Reading: Informational Text
RL	= Reading: Literature
RF	= Reading: Foundation Skills
SL	= Speaking and Listening

+ +

Strand Reading: Foundational Skills
Substrand Phonics and Word Recognition
ELA.RF.5.3: Units 1–22

Strand Reading: Foundational Skills
Substrand Fluency
ELA.RF.5.4: Units 1–22

+ +

Strand Reading: Informational Text
Substrand Key Ideas and Details
ELA.RI.5.1: Units 1–22
ELA.RI.5.2: Units 1–22
ELA.RI.5.3: Units 1–5, 7–13, 15–16, 18–20

Strand Reading: Informational Text
Substrand Craft and Structure
ELA.RI.5.4: Units 1–22
ELA.RI.5.5: Units 7, 10–12,
ELA.RI.5.6: Units 7–8, 10–12, 19

Strand Reading: Informational Text
Substrand Integration of Knowledge and Ideas
ELA.RI.5.7: Units 1–19
ELA.RI.5.8: Units 1–22
ELA.RI.5.9: Units 1–19

Strand Reading: Informational Text
Substrand Range of Reading and Level of Text Complexity
ELA.RI.5.10: Units 1–22

+ +

Strand Reading: Literature
Substrand Key Ideas and Details
ELA.RL.5.1: Units 2, 4–6, 8, 10, 12, 14, 16, 18, 20, 22
ELA.RL.5.2: Units 2, 4, 6, 8, 10, 12, 14, 16, 18, 20, 22
ELA.RL.5.3: Units 2, 4–6, 8, 10, 12, 14, 16, 18, 20, 22

+ +

Strand Reading: Literature   **Substrand** Craft and Structure

ELA.RL.5.4: Units 2, 4–6, 8, 10, 12, 14, 16, 18, 20, 22
ELA.RL.5.5: Units 2, 4–6, 8, 10, 12, 14, 16, 18, 20, 22
ELA.RL.5.6: Units 12–13

Strand Reading: Literature   **Substrand** Integration of Knowledge and Ideas

ELA.RL.5.9: Units 10, 18

Strand Reading: Literature   **Substrand** Range of Reading and Level of Text Complexity

ELA.RL.5.10: Units 2, 4–6, 8, 10, 12, 14, 16, 18, 20, 22

+ +

Strand Speaking and Listening   **Substrand** Comprehension and Collaboration

ELA.SL.5.1: Units 1–22
ELA.SL.5.3: Units 7, 11, 16–18, 20–22

Strand Speaking and Listening   **Substrand** Presentation of Knowledge and Ideas

ELA.SL.5.4: Units 7, 11, 16–18, 20–22
ELA.SL.5.6: Units 21–22

+ +

Strand Writing   **Substrand** Text Types and Purposes

ELA.W.5.1: Units 1–20
ELA.W.5.2: Units 1–20
ELA.W.5.3: Units 3–4, 6–7, 13, 17, 19

Strand Writing   **Substrand** Production and Distribution of Writing

ELA.W.5.4: Units 1–20

Strand Writing   **Substrand** Research to Build and Present Knowledge

ELA.W.5.7: Units 1–20
ELA.W.5.8: Units 1–20
ELA.W.5.9: Units 1–20

Strand Writing   **Substrand** Range of Writing

ELA.W.5.10: Units 1–20

+ +

Strand Language   **Substrand** Conventions of Standard English

ELA.L.5.1: Units 1–22
ELA.L.5.2: Units 1–22

Strand Language   **Substrand** Knowledge of Language

ELA.L.5.3: Units 1–22

Strand Language   **Substrand** Vocabulary Acquisition and Use

ELA.L.5.4: Units 1–22
ELA.L.5.5: Units 1–22
ELA.L.5.6: Units 1–22
